One Book to Rule It All. Copyright © 2024 Lisa Brown

ISBN: 978-91-89848-99-3

All Rights Reserved. No part of this work may be reproduced, incorporated into a computer system, or transmitted in any form or by any means (electronic, mechanical, photocopying, recording or otherwise) without the prior written permission of the copyright holders. Infringement of such rights may constitute an intellectual property crime.

ONE BOOK TO RULE IT ALL

**THE COMPLETE GUIDE TO
PERSONAL GROWTH**

Lisa Brown

The Beginning of Your Transformation   7

Mindset and Personal Growth

Take Control of Your Life and Unleash Your Unlimited Potential   13

Achieving Personal and Professional Effectiveness Through Universal Habits   20

How Tiny Daily Changes Lead to Big Results Over Time   26

Live Fully in the Present for Inner Peace and Happiness   33

Change Your Thinking to Live a Happier and Fuller Life   40

Identifying and Eliminating Self-Destructive Thought Patterns   47

Be Kind to Yourself – The Power of Self-Compassion   55

Success and Productivity

Ignite Your Burning Desire and Unshakeable Belief   68

The Secret Formula for Success—Talent, Effort, and Opportunity   76

Unlock Your Potential with NLP   85

The Science of Success: How to Apply Proven Principles to Achieve Greatness   93

Positive Attitude and Emotional Management for a Full Life   102

The Power of Belief and Consistent Action   110

Resilience and Faith — The Unbreakable Combination to Overcome Adversity   119

Why Financial Education Matters	127
Balancing Material Success and Spiritual Fulfillment	135
Unlock Your Inner Power	143
Mastering the Art of Caring Less: Focus on What Really Matters	149
The 80/20 Rule: Maximize Your Results with Less Effort	156

Relationships and Communication

The Power of People Skills	168
Four Simple Principles to Live a Free and Happy Life	177
Vulnerability: Living with Courage and Authenticity	185
Identifying and Distancing Yourself from Toxic People	193

Spirituality and Wellness

Embrace Change to Thrive in a Constantly Evolving World	207
The Journey is the Reward	214
The Road to Your Own Treasure	222
Spiritual Principles for Success and Fulfillment	229
The Healing Power of Your Mind	237
The Transformative Power of Your Mind and Positive Affirmations	245
The Joy in Everyday Moments	253
The Journey Within – Discovering Yourself to Find Freedom	260

The Beginning of Your Journey	268
A Personalized Action Plan	272

1
The Beginning of Your Transformation

You've just taken the first step toward transforming your life. This isn't just another book—it's your guide to unlocking the potential that's already within you. Each page is filled with the wisdom distilled from some of the greatest minds in personal development, offering you the tools to create lasting change. As you read, you'll uncover the secrets to mastering your mindset, building powerful habits, and finding true fulfillment in all areas of life. Get ready, because this journey is about to get exciting.

Have you ever wondered what it takes to truly change your life? Not just to tweak a few habits here and there but to experience a deep, meaningful transformation? This book will show you exactly that—how to shift your mindset, unlock your hidden potential, and take concrete steps toward the life you've always dreamed of. Whether you're striving for success, better relationships, or simply a deeper sense of happiness and purpose, what lies ahead will guide you every step of the way.

We're going to learn how to harness the power of your mind, how to overcome limiting beliefs that have held you back for years, and how to tap into the infinite potential within you that's been lying dormant. You'll discover the secrets of resilience—how to bounce back from setbacks stronger than ever before. We'll explore the art of goal-setting and how to turn your dreams into achievable milestones. And, most importantly, we'll look at how to cultivate a life of balance, joy, and fulfillment, drawing from practices that nourish not only your mind but your spirit as well.

Throughout this book, we'll explore key themes that will guide you on your personal growth journey. You'll discover how your mindset plays a powerful role in shaping your reality, learning how to rewire your thoughts for success, peace, and joy. We'll explore the science behind habits—those small, consistent actions that, over time, lead to significant results in your life.

Emotional mastery will be another focus, teaching you how to navigate your emotions rather than letting them control you, helping you create a lasting sense of inner calm. We'll also look at goal-setting and manifestation, breaking down the steps to set goals that align with your values and turn them into reality.

Resilience and grit will show you how to view challenges and failures as opportunities for growth, with persistence becoming your greatest ally. And we'll explore spiritual fulfillment, helping you connect with something greater than yourself, tapping into your purpose, and finding inner peace along the way.

Each of these themes will help you build the life you desire, equipping you with the tools to create real change and lasting fulfillment. This book is structured to give you real tools that you can start applying right away. It's not about abstract theories but practical steps that will lead to tangible changes in your life. And here's the best part: the knowledge you'll gain is not just a random collection of ideas. It's drawn from the greatest minds in personal development—people like Napoleon Hill, Brené Brown, Louise Hay, and many others whose work has transformed millions of lives across the world.

But don't just read passively. Engage with what's here. Apply it. Let it inspire you, push you out of your comfort zone, and challenge you to grow. If you're willing to fully invest in this journey, you won't be the same person by the time you finish this book.

Right now, you're at the start of something exciting. A new chapter of your life. What's possible for you is far beyond what you can imagine right now. So buckle up—because together, we're about to unlock the incredible potential inside you.

Your journey toward a life of purpose, joy, and success starts now. Are you ready? Let's go!

I
Mindset and Personal Growth

Welcome to the first part of your journey toward self-improvement! Personal development is the foundation upon which you build a fulfilling and successful life. In this section, we'll explore the importance of cultivating effective habits, setting meaningful goals, and embracing a growth mindset. You'll discover practical strategies to enhance your daily routines and unlock your full potential.

Before diving into the content, take a moment to reflect on your current approach to personal development with the following self-assessment questionnaire. This will help you identify your strengths and areas for growth as you embark on this transformative journey.

Personal Development and Habits Self-Assessment

Check the box next to the response that best describes your current approach to personal development and habits. Be honest—this is your personal journey!

1. How often do you set personal goals for yourself?

☐ A. I regularly set and review my goals.

☐ B. I set goals occasionally but don't always track them.

☐ C. I rarely set goals and often feel directionless.

2. How consistent are you with your daily habits?

☐ A. I have a solid routine and stick to it consistently.

☐ B. I have some habits but struggle to maintain them.

☐ C. I often lack structure in my daily habits.

3. How do you respond to challenges or setbacks in your personal growth?

☐ A. I view challenges as opportunities to learn and grow.

☐ B. I try to learn from setbacks but can feel discouraged.

☐ C. I often feel defeated and struggle to bounce back.

4. How frequently do you engage in self-reflection?

☐ A. I reflect regularly and use insights to improve myself.

☐ B. I reflect occasionally but could do more.

☐ C. I rarely take time to reflect on my thoughts and actions.

5. How open are you to trying new habits or approaches to improve yourself?

☐ A. I love experimenting with new techniques and ideas.

☐ B. I'm open to new approaches but hesitant to change.

☐ C. I prefer to stick with what I know and avoid trying new things.

6. How do you prioritize self-care in your daily routine?

☐ A. I make self-care a priority and incorporate it into my routine.

☐ B. I try to include self-care, but it's not consistent.

☐ C. I often neglect self-care and feel drained.

7. How do you handle negative thoughts about yourself?

☐ A. I actively challenge and reframe negative thoughts.

☐ B. I recognize them but struggle to change my mindset.

☐ C. I often accept negative thoughts as truths.

Reflection & Next Steps

Mostly A's: You have a strong foundation in personal development and consistently work on your habits. The upcoming chapters will provide you with new strategies and insights to deepen your practice and inspire further growth.

Mostly B's: You're on the right path, but there's room for improvement. This section will offer valuable insights and techniques to refine your habits and boost your personal development.

Mostly C's: It appears you may be facing challenges in your personal growth. This section will guide you through essential principles and actionable steps to empower you on your journey toward self-improvement and habit formation. You'll learn essential concepts and strategies that will empower you to take control of your personal development,

Embrace the journey ahead!

2
Take Control of Your Life and Unleash Your Unlimited Potential

Do you ever feel like there's something more you could be doing with your life, but you just don't know how to tap into it? It's easy to get caught up in the daily grind—going through the motions, reacting to whatever life throws at you, and putting your own dreams on hold. But here's the truth: You have way more power and potential than you realize. The key to unlocking that potential and taking control of your life isn't found in external circumstances—it's inside of you, just waiting to be awakened.

The Power of Decisions: Where It All Begins

Everything in your life—from where you live to what you do, even down to how you feel daily—is the result of your decisions. This may seem obvious, but think about it for a second: Your decisions shape your destiny. Whether you realize it or not, every little choice you make, like what to focus on or how to spend your time, sets a direction for your future.

Too often, we let life happen to us instead of actively choosing what we want. We say things like, "I'll start working on that dream once things calm down," or, "If only I had more time, money, or support, then I could make a change." But here's the thing: You're in control right now. No one is coming to save you or give you permission to start living your best life. It's up to you to take charge and start making decisions that align with the person you want to become.

Change Your Focus, Change Your Life

One of the most powerful tools you have is your ability to control your focus. Where focus goes, energy flows. If you're constantly focusing on what's wrong or what you don't have, you'll stay stuck in that negative mindset. On the other hand, if you train yourself to focus on what you want to achieve and the possibilities ahead, you'll start seeing opportunities everywhere.

Here's how it works: when you focus on a problem, your brain looks for more problems. It's a survival mechanism, but in today's world, it often holds us back. To unlock your potential, you need to shift your focus from problems to solutions. This doesn't mean ignoring challenges; it means framing them in a way that empowers you to take action. Start asking yourself empowering questions like, "How can I use this situation to grow?" or, "What's one small step I can take today to move closer to my goals?"

When you make this shift, you'll notice a dramatic difference in how you feel and how you approach obstacles. You'll start thinking creatively, coming up with new ideas, and feeling more in control.

Emotional Mastery: How to Take Control of Your Feelings

If you want to take control of your life, you need to take control of your emotions. The problem is, most people think emotions are something that just happen to them, like the weather—some days it's sunny, and other days it's stormy. But the truth is, you can choose how you feel.

Your emotions are the result of three things: your focus (what you're thinking about), your physiology (how you're using your body), and the meaning you give to events. Let's break these down:

- **Focus**: As we just talked about, where you place your attention determines your emotional state. If you focus on what's missing or what you can't control, you'll feel frustrated or anxious. Shift your focus to what you're grateful for or the positive steps you can take, and your emotional state will shift too.
- **Physiology**: Your body language and posture play a huge role in how you feel. Think about it: when you're feeling down, how do you sit or stand? Chances are, you slouch, your shoulders are

hunched, and your breathing is shallow. To instantly change your mood, change your posture. Stand up straight, take deep breaths, and move with energy. It's amazing how a simple shift in how you use your body can change your emotions in an instant.

- **Meaning**: The meaning you attach to events shapes how you experience them. Two people can go through the same situation and have completely different reactions based on the story they tell themselves. When something happens, ask yourself, "What else could this mean?" By choosing empowering meanings, you change how you feel about any situation.

Break the Cycle: Defeat Limiting Beliefs

One of the biggest things holding people back is their own limiting beliefs. These are the stories you tell yourself about what you can or can't do. Maybe you believe you're not smart enough, or that success is for other people, or that it's too late to make a change. But here's the reality: Your beliefs shape your reality.

If you believe something is impossible, your mind will find all the reasons why it's true. But if you believe something is possible, you'll start looking for ways to make it happen. It all starts with your mindset.

So how do you break free from limiting beliefs? Start by questioning them. Ask yourself, "Is this really true?" and "Where did this belief come from?" Often, limiting beliefs are things you picked up from your environment—parents, teachers, society—but they're not facts. You have the power to rewrite the script.

Next, create new, empowering beliefs that align with the life you want to live. Instead of thinking, "I'm not good enough," tell yourself, "I have everything I need to succeed." Repeat these new beliefs daily until they become your default way of thinking.

Consistent Action: The Key to Unlocking Your Potential

All the mindset shifts in the world won't do much if you don't take action. This is where most people get stuck—they get inspired, but they don't follow through. To truly awaken your potential, you need to take consistent, massive action.

Here's the thing: You don't need to have it all figured out. You just need to start. The biggest mistake people make is waiting until everything is perfect before they act. Perfectionism is just another form of procrastination. Instead, focus on progress, not perfection.

You have the power to rewrite the script.

Action creates momentum. The more you do, the more confident you become, and the easier it gets to keep moving forward. Don't worry about making the right decision every time—just make a decision and adjust along the way. As long as you're moving in the direction of your goals, you're on the right track.

Practical Exercises to Awaken Your Potential

Here are some simple but powerful exercises you can do to start taking control of your life and unlocking your potential:

Create Your Vision

Spend 10 minutes writing down what your ideal life looks like. Be specific—what do you want to achieve, who do you want to become, and how do you want to feel? Keep this vision somewhere you can see it daily and use it as your guide for making decisions.

Shift Your Focus Daily

Every morning, write down three things you're grateful for and three things you want to focus on that day. This simple practice helps train your mind to look for opportunities and solutions rather than problems.

Practice Power Poses

For the next week, whenever you're feeling low energy or stressed, stand up tall, roll your shoulders back, and take deep breaths for two minutes. Notice how this simple change in posture can instantly shift your emotional state.

Identify Limiting Beliefs

Take a few minutes to write down any beliefs that are holding you back. Then, challenge each belief by asking, "Is this really true?" For each limiting belief, write down a new empowering belief that aligns with the person you want to become.

Take One Bold Action

Identify one area of your life where you've been holding back or waiting for the "perfect moment." Take one bold action today, whether it's sending that email, making that phone call, or starting that project. Don't overthink it—just take action.

▶ Immediate Action: Create Your Personal Empowerment Statement

To start taking control of your life and tapping into your unlimited potential, take a moment to create a Personal Empowerment Statement. This statement should encapsulate your values, goals, and the mindset you wish to adopt moving forward.

Steps to Create Your Personal Empowerment Statement:

Reflect on Your Values: What matters most to you? Think about the core values that guide your decisions and actions. Examples might include integrity, growth, creativity, or service.

Identify Your Goals: Write down your short-term and long-term goals. Be specific about what you want to achieve in different areas of your life, such as career, relationships, health, and personal growth.

Craft Your Statement: Combine your values and goals into a powerful statement that resonates with you. For example: "I am committed to living a life of integrity and growth, pursuing my dreams fearlessly and positively impacting those around me."

Make it Visual: Write your statement down in bold letters and decorate it. Place it somewhere you'll see it daily—on your bathroom mirror, as your phone wallpaper, or in your journal.

Questions for Reflection

- What is one decision you've been avoiding that could significantly impact your life? What is holding you back from making it?

- How often do you take control of where your focus goes throughout the day? What would change if you consistently focused on possibilities rather than problems?

- Which limiting beliefs have shaped your life so far, and how would your actions differ if you no longer believed those limitations?

- How do you currently manage your emotions in challenging situations? What small changes in your physiology or perspective could help you gain more emotional control?

- What bold action can you take today that would move you closer to the person you want to become, even if it's uncomfortable?

Conclusion

By taking control of your focus, mastering your emotions, and breaking through limiting beliefs, you can unleash the giant within you. The power to create the life you want is already inside of you—you just need to take the first step and keep moving forward. It's not about achieving everything all at once but consistently taking action toward your goals. Over time, those small actions will compound, and you'll awaken to the incredible potential you've always had.

Final Reflection

Every decision, every moment of focus, every emotion you choose to master shapes your future. The life you dream of is within your reach, but it requires one thing: action.

3

Achieving Personal and Professional Effectiveness Through Universal Habits

We all want to be more effective in life, whether it's at work, in relationships, or when striving to meet personal goals. But effectiveness isn't working harder or running ourselves into the ground; it's working smarter, using our energy and time wisely, and aligning ourselves with principles that hold true, no matter the situation. These principles aren't just short-term tricks or life hacks, they're timeless values that, when integrated into daily habits, lead to consistent results and long-term success.

So, how do you become highly effective in all areas of life? The key lies in developing a set of habits that are grounded in universal principles—principles like responsibility, integrity, patience, and growth. Let's explore how these habits work and how you can begin applying them today.

Take Full Responsibility for Your Life

The first step to becoming more effective is realizing that you are responsible for your life. This means understanding that, while you can't always control what happens to you, you can control how you respond. The idea is simple: be proactive, not reactive. Stop blaming others, the economy, or your past for where you are today. Start owning your choices and recognize that you always have the power to change your situation by choosing how to respond to it.

Let's say you're dealing with a difficult boss or challenging work environment. You could complain and let your frustration boil over, but that puts the power outside yourself. Instead, take proactive steps: Can you have a constructive conversation? Are there skills you can develop to navigate the situation better? The proactive approach focuses on what you can do, rather than what's being done to you.

Recognize that you always have the power to change your situation by choosing how to respond to it.

Begin with the End in Mind

Effective people don't drift through life, reacting to whatever comes their way. They have a clear vision of what they want to achieve. It's like using a GPS—if you don't know where you're headed, how will you ever get there? This doesn't mean just having a career goal in mind, but also envisioning the type of person you want to be and the life you want to live.

Ask yourself: What kind of legacy do I want to leave? How do I want my relationships to look? Where do I want my career to take me? Once you have this clarity, your daily decisions start aligning with your bigger picture. When you know where you want to go, you can reverse-engineer the steps needed to get there.

Prioritize What Matters Most

It's easy to get lost in the busy-ness of life—meetings, emails, social media, and countless little tasks that feel urgent but aren't really important. Effective people know how to prioritize. They focus on the activities that will give them the biggest return in the long run, rather than simply reacting to what feels urgent in the moment.

To do this, think about what's important versus what's urgent. Urgent tasks demand immediate attention but might not contribute to your bigger goals, like answering emails or dealing with a minor work crisis. Important tasks, like investing in relationships or working on your skills, often don't have immediate deadlines but have a massive impact over time. The trick is learning to say "no" to the urgent, so you can focus on the important.

Seek Win-Win Solutions

Effective people understand that success isn't about competition, but collaboration. They aim for solutions where both sides benefit, creating mutually satisfying outcomes. Whether you're negotiating at work or resolving a personal conflict, always look for ways where both parties can come out better.

This mindset not only fosters better relationships but also leads to more sustainable success. You don't have to step on others to get ahead; instead, think about how everyone can win. This is the essence of building lasting, meaningful relationships both professionally and personally.

Understand Before Trying to Be Understood

One of the most powerful ways to improve effectiveness in relationships, whether at work or at home, is through empathy. We often rush to get our point across without truly understanding the other person. But the truth is, when you make the effort to understand someone else's perspective first, they are much more likely to listen to and understand yours.

Next time you're in a conversation, especially during a disagreement, focus fully on what the other person is saying. Don't plan your response while they're talking. Ask questions, dig deeper, and really listen. When people feel heard and understood, they become more open and solutions come more naturally.

Continually Sharpen Your Skills

No matter how effective you become, there's always room for improvement. Highly effective people dedicate time to continuous learning and self-improvement. Whether it's enhancing your professional skills, taking care of your mental and physical health, or developing emotionally, growth never stops.

Set aside time regularly for self-care and self-development. Read, meditate, exercise, learn new skills. By investing in yourself, you not only maintain your current effectiveness, but you also expand your capacity for even greater success.

Practical Exercises to Build Effectiveness

Here are some actionable exercises to help you start incorporating these principles into your life:

Create a Personal Responsibility Map

Write down situations in your life where you feel stuck or frustrated. Next to each one, list out specific actions you can take to improve or resolve the situation. This exercise helps you shift from reactive to proactive thinking.

Weekly Prioritization Review

At the start of each week, list all your tasks. Then, categorize them into "urgent" and "important." Make sure you schedule time for the important activities that align with your long-term goals, even if they aren't urgent.

Win-Win Mindset Challenge

Identify a current conflict or negotiation in your life. Approach the other party and propose a solution that benefits both of you. Focus on creating a collaborative, not competitive, environment.

Empathy Listening Practice

In your next conversation, commit to listening more than you speak. Avoid interrupting or preparing your response while the other person is talking. Ask clarifying questions and repeat what they've said to ensure you truly understand.

Skill-Building Plan

Choose one area of your life—physical health, professional skills, or emotional intelligence—where you want to improve. Set a clear, measurable goal (e.g., run 3 times a week, take an online course, or meditate daily) and track your progress over the next month.

▸ Immediate Action: The Power of One Habit

Developing personal and professional effectiveness starts with creating intentional habits. To see immediate progress, choose one habit you want to implement or improve. This habit should align with your goals and have the potential to create a positive ripple effect across different areas of your life.

Steps to Implement Your Universal Habit:

Identify the Habit: What's one habit that, if practiced consistently, would improve your personal or professional life? Examples might be:

- Waking up an hour earlier to have quiet, focused time.
- Blocking out 30 minutes a day for learning or skill development.
- Practicing gratitude each morning.

Set a Clear Intention: Write down exactly what you plan to do and when. Be specific: "I will spend 10 minutes meditating every morning after I wake up," or "I will read 20 pages of a personal development book every night before bed."

Start Small: To make the habit stick, keep it small and manageable. Focus on consistency rather than perfection. Set an achievable target, such as starting with just 5 minutes of journaling or taking a 10-minute walk during lunch.

Track Your Progress: Keep a journal or use a habit-tracking app to mark off each day you successfully complete the habit. Even a simple checkmark on a calendar can create a sense of accomplishment.

Questions for Reflection

- In what areas of your life are you currently reacting rather than proactively taking responsibility? How can you begin to shift your mindset to take control of those situations?

- How clear is your vision of the life you want to create? What steps can you take to refine and align your daily actions with that vision?

- What tasks in your life are "urgent" but not necessarily "important"? How can you re-prioritize to focus on what truly matters for long-term success?

- How often do you approach conflicts with a win-win mindset? What would change in your relationships if you consistently sought solutions that benefit both parties?

Conclusion

By consistently applying these principles and habits, you'll notice a significant improvement in both your personal and professional life. Effectiveness is developing deep, meaningful habits that align with universal truths. It's a journey, but one that's well worth taking.

Final Reflection

The power to become who you aspire to be lies in the actions you take every single day.

4

How Tiny Daily Changes Lead to Big Results Over Time

Have you ever wondered why it feels so hard to stick to big goals? Maybe you've set out to lose weight, start a business, or finally write that novel, but after a few days or weeks, your motivation fizzled out. It's not that you don't have the drive or the talent—it's just that you're probably approaching it all wrong. The truth is, the path to success isn't about making massive leaps forward; it's about taking tiny, consistent steps. Small, daily changes, even ones that seem insignificant, can lead to life-changing results over time. Let's dig into how this works and how you can start applying it to your life today.

Why Small Habits Matter More Than Big Goals

It's tempting to think that to achieve something great, you need to make a radical change. But the reality is, small habits compound. Imagine if you got just 1% better at something every day. That seems tiny, right? But over a year, that 1% improvement adds up to a 37% increase! It's the power of compounding, and it works the same way for personal growth as it does for money.

Think about brushing your teeth. It's such a small habit that you probably don't even think about it, but imagine what your dental health would look like if you skipped it for months. The same principle applies to other areas of your life: tiny habits, repeated consistently, have a powerful cumulative effect.

Here's the key: You don't need to overhaul your life overnight to see big results. You just need to focus on getting 1% better every day. Whether it's fitness, personal development, or financial goals, it's these small, often unnoticed actions that lead to massive transformation.

The Importance of Identity: Becoming the Person Who Does the Things You Want to Do

If you want lasting change, you need to start with your identity, not your goals. Here's what I mean: It's easier to stick with habits when they are part of who you are, not just what you want to achieve. For example, if you see yourself as a "runner," it's a lot easier to run regularly than if you're someone who is "trying to run more."

Instead of setting goals like, "I want to lose 20 pounds" or "I want to save $10,000," focus on who you want to become. If you want to lose weight, adopt the identity of a healthy person—someone who values fitness and makes healthy choices naturally. If you want to build wealth, start seeing yourself as someone who is financially savvy and disciplined.

When your actions align with your identity, you stop thinking about them as tasks to complete and start seeing them as part of who you are. You become the kind of person who runs, who saves, who writes—because that's just what you do.

The Habit Loop: How to Build Habits That Stick

There's a simple loop that drives all habits: Cue, Craving, Response, and Reward. Understanding this loop is key to building habits that last.

- **Cue**: This is what triggers the habit. It could be a time of day, a location, an emotion, or something else that starts the behavior. For example, walking into the kitchen might cue you to grab a snack.
- **Craving**: This is the desire or motivation behind the habit. You don't just eat a snack because you walked into the kitchen—you eat because you're craving the reward of feeling full or tasting something sweet.
- **Response**: This is the actual habit or action you perform. It's the behavior triggered by the cue and driven by the craving.

- **Reward**: This is the benefit you get from completing the habit. It's what reinforces the loop, making you want to repeat the habit in the future.

To build good habits, you need to work with this loop. Start by choosing a cue that triggers your desired habit. For example, if you want to start exercising, make putting on your workout clothes the cue. Then, ensure there's a reward that makes you feel good after completing the habit, like enjoying a smoothie after your workout or giving yourself some time to relax.

You can also stack habits by attaching a new habit to one you already do regularly. This technique is called "habit stacking." If you already brush your teeth every morning (which you probably do!), you can attach a new habit to it, like doing 10 squats right afterward. Over time, the new habit becomes just as automatic as brushing your teeth.

The Power of Environment: Shape Your Surroundings for Success

If you're trying to build new habits, the environment you're in plays a huge role. Your surroundings can either support your habits or sabotage them. Want to eat healthier? Keep fruit on the counter and hide the junk food in the back of the cupboard. Want to write more? Create a space that feels inspiring to work in and remove distractions like your phone.

We often think willpower is the key to success, but it's actually easier to design your environment so that you don't have to rely on willpower as much. When you make good habits the path of least resistance—and bad habits harder to do—you'll naturally start doing more of what benefits you.

The Long-Term Mindset: Focus on Consistency Over Perfection

One of the biggest mistakes people make when building habits is expecting perfection. Here's the thing: you're going to mess up. You'll skip a workout, eat junk food, or procrastinate on a task. That's normal! The goal isn't perfection—it's consistency over the long term.

If you miss a day, don't beat yourself up. Just get back on track the next day. Missing once won't derail you, but if you let it snowball into missing two or three times, it becomes a problem. The key is to never miss twice in a row. Forgive yourself for slip-ups, and focus on getting back into the routine as quickly as possible.

The goal isn't perfection—it is consistency over the long term.

Practical Exercises to Start Making Tiny Daily Changes

Now let's put that knowledge into action. Here are some exercises to help you apply these principles:

Start Small and Choose One Tiny Habit

Pick one area of your life where you want to see improvement. Break down a goal into the smallest possible habit you can start today. For example, if you want to exercise more, your habit might be as small as doing two push-ups a day. The key is to start so small that it feels almost effortless to do it.

Habit Stacking

Identify a habit you already do every day, like making coffee in the morning or brushing your teeth. Then, stack a new habit onto it. For instance, after you brush your teeth, you could spend one minute journaling, or after making coffee, you could do a quick stretch.

Design Your Environment

Think about the habit you want to build and create an environment that supports it. If you want to read more, place a book on your pillow every morning so it's waiting for you at night. If you want to eat healthier, prep fruits and veggies in advance and make them easily accessible in your fridge.

Track Your Progress

Use a simple habit tracker, like a calendar or app, to mark off each day you complete your habit. This visual cue keeps you motivated and shows you how small actions add up over time.

The Two-Minute Rule

Whatever habit you want to build, start by doing it for just two minutes a day. This gets you in the habit of showing up, which is half the battle. Over time, you can gradually increase the time and effort you put in, but for now, just focus on consistency.

▶ Immediate Action: Identify Your 1% Change

One of the most powerful ways to create lasting change in your life is by focusing on making small, incremental improvements—what we call the 1% change. These are tiny adjustments that, over time, create significant results.

Steps to Implement Your 1% Change:

Pick One Area of Life: Identify a specific area where you'd like to see improvement. This could be related to your health, relationships, finances, or personal growth. For example, you might want to improve your fitness, deepen your connections with loved ones, or become more organized.

Choose a 1% Change: Think of a small, easy-to-do action that you can repeat daily. Keep it simple—this should be something you can commit to without too much effort. Examples could include:

- Drinking one extra glass of water each day.
- Sending a thoughtful message to someone you care about every morning.
- Decluttering one small area of your house for 5 minutes each day.

Commit to Consistency: The key to tiny daily changes is doing them consistently. Choose a specific time or trigger that will remind you to take this small action. For example, drink your extra glass of water with lunch, or set a daily alarm to text someone you appreciate.

Start a log of your 1% change: Each day, write down what you did and how you feel about it. Even if the change feels small at first, tracking it will help you notice the cumulative impact over time.

Questions for Reflection

- In what areas of your life have you tried to make massive changes, only to lose motivation? How might breaking those changes into tiny, daily habits help you stay consistent?
- What small, 1% improvements can you start making today that would lead to significant growth in the long term?
- How does your current identity align with the habits you want to build? What shifts in your self-image would make those habits feel more natural and sustainable?
- What environmental changes can you make to support the habits you want to develop? Are there any distractions you can remove to make it easier to focus on your goals?
- How can you apply the "habit stacking" technique to your existing routine? Which current habits can serve as anchors for new behaviors?
- What is your attitude toward perfectionism in habit-building? How can you shift your mindset to prioritize long-term

consistency over flawless execution?

Conclusion

By embracing the power of tiny, consistent changes, you'll be surprised at how much you can achieve over time. The path to success is making steady progress, one small step at a time. Stick with it, and over the months and years, you'll find yourself far ahead of where you started.

Final Reflection

Every monumental change begins with a small, almost imperceptible action.

5

Live Fully in the Present for Inner Peace and Happiness

We often hear the phrase "live in the moment," but what does that really mean? In our fast-paced world, we're usually either worrying about the future or reliving the past. Maybe you're stressing about next week's deadlines, or maybe you're replaying that awkward conversation from yesterday in your head. Sound familiar? What if I told you that this constant mental chatter is the very thing keeping you from experiencing true peace and happiness? The good news is that there's a way out, and it's simpler than you might think: living fully in the present.

Living in the present means shifting your focus away from the endless "what ifs" and "should have beens" and anchoring yourself in the now. When you learn to do this, something amazing happens: the noise in your mind quiets down, and you start to feel a deep sense of calm and clarity. That's when real happiness starts to emerge—not the fleeting kind based on external circumstances, but a lasting peace that comes from within.

Why the Present Moment Is All You Really Have

Here's a simple but powerful truth: the only real moment you have is this one. The past is gone, and the future hasn't happened yet. Sure, you can think about them, but they only exist as thoughts in your mind. The present is the only time you can actually live. It's where your life is unfolding.

Yet, we spend so much time anywhere but here. We're either dwelling on past mistakes or anxiously planning for what's next. This constant tug-of-war between the past and the future robs us of the peace and joy that come from being fully engaged in the present.

Imagine you're out for a walk on a beautiful day. The sun is shining, there's a gentle breeze, and the world feels alive. But instead of enjoying the moment, you're stuck in your head, worrying about tomorrow's to-do list or replaying an argument you had last week. You're physically present, but mentally absent. You're missing life.

When you live in the present, life becomes richer. You notice the details, feel more connected to yourself and the world around you, and experience a sense of ease and flow. You stop resisting what is and start accepting things as they come. This is where inner peace begins.

How the Mind Gets in the Way

Here's the tricky part: your mind doesn't want to live in the present. It loves to keep you busy with thoughts about the past or the future. It's constantly pulling you into stories—some real, most imagined—that keep you distracted. The mind likes to analyze, predict, and plan because it believes that by doing so, it can control everything. But let's face it: the mind is terrible at predicting the future, and it can't change the past.

> *The present is the only time you can actually live.*

Yet, we often get caught in what's called "psychological time"—where instead of experiencing life as it happens, we let our thoughts dominate. We tell ourselves stories like, "I'll be happy when I get that promotion," or "If only I hadn't made that mistake years ago, things would be different now." This way of thinking puts happiness on hold and keeps us trapped in a cycle of dissatisfaction.

The mind isn't the enemy—it's just doing what it's wired to do. But you can learn to recognize when it's pulling you out of the present and gently guide yourself back. The more you practice, the more natural it becomes to let go of unnecessary thoughts and stay rooted in the here and now.

The Power of Presence: How It Transforms Your Life

When you start living fully in the present, everything changes. Your relationships improve because you're truly there with the people around you, not distracted by your phone or lost in your thoughts. You become more productive because you're focused on the task at hand rather than multitasking or worrying about what comes next. Most importantly, you start to feel a deep sense of peace and happiness that comes from simply being, rather than always doing.

Presence also helps you handle challenges more effectively. When you're fully in the present, you're better equipped to respond to life's ups and downs without overreacting. Instead of getting caught up in a spiral of worry or frustration, you can approach problems with a calm, clear mind. You see things for what they are, not what you fear they might become.

And here's the magic of it: when you're fully present, even the simplest things in life become more enjoyable. A meal, a conversation, or a walk in the park—things you might normally rush through—become opportunities for joy and connection. Life becomes an experience, not a race.

Practical Ways to Start Living in the Now

So, how do you actually start living in the present? It's not something you can flip on like a light switch, but with practice, it becomes easier. Here are some simple, practical steps to help you anchor yourself in the moment and experience the power of now.

Practice Mindful Breathing. Your breath is always in the present—it's your anchor to the now. Anytime you feel your mind racing or drifting, take a moment to focus on your breathing. Inhale slowly, feel the air fill your lungs, and then exhale, letting go of any tension. Even just a few deep breaths can bring you back to the present.

Notice Your Surroundings. When you catch yourself lost in thought, use your senses to bring yourself back. What do you see around you? What sounds can you hear? How does the air feel on your skin? By tuning into your senses, you ground yourself in the current moment and give your mind something tangible to focus on.

Let Go of Time. Try not to think of your day in terms of "what's next" or "what should have happened." Instead, focus on what you're doing right now. Whether you're washing the dishes, having a conversation, or working on a project, give it your full attention. Let go of the need to rush through things and simply be present with whatever you're doing.

Recognize Thought Patterns. The next time you feel anxious or stressed, pause and ask yourself, "Where is my mind right now?" You'll probably notice that you're thinking about the past or the future. Once you recognize this, gently bring yourself back to the present by focusing on your breathing or your surroundings.

Accept What Is. A huge part of living in the present is accepting things as they are, without resistance. That doesn't mean you don't work to improve your life or fix problems, it means you stop fighting reality. When you accept the present moment, even if it's uncomfortable, you reduce suffering. Practice saying to yourself, "This is where I am right now, and that's okay."

Exercises to Help You Live in the Present

To help you fully integrate the practice of living in the now into your daily life, here are a few exercises you can try:

The Five Senses Check-In

Every day, take a few minutes to do a five senses check-in. Sit comfortably and focus on what you can see, hear, touch, taste, and smell. This simple exercise grounds you in the present and helps train your mind to focus on what's happening right now.

Daily Mindfulness Practice

Set aside 5-10 minutes each morning to practice mindfulness. This practice strengthens your ability to stay present throughout the day.

Mindful Walking

The next time you take a walk, leave your phone behind and focus on the sensations of walking. Feel the ground beneath your feet, notice the rhythm of your steps, and take in the sights and sounds around you. This turns an ordinary walk into a meditative practice and helps you stay rooted in the present.

Gratitude Journal

At the end of each day, write down three things you're grateful for. Focusing on gratitude pulls you out of negative thought patterns and reminds you to appreciate the present moment. Over time, this simple habit will help you cultivate a more positive and present-focused mindset.

▶ Immediate Action: The 5-Minute Mindfulness Practice

One of the most powerful ways to cultivate inner peace and happiness is to train your mind to stay present. Here's a simple exercise that you can implement immediately to practice living fully in the moment.

Steps for Your 5-Minute Mindfulness Practice:

Find a Quiet Space: Sit comfortably in a quiet space where you won't be interrupted for five minutes. You don't need anything fancy—just a chair, a cushion, or even sitting on the floor will work.

Focus on Your Breathing: Close your eyes and take a few deep breaths. Pay attention to how the air feels as it enters and leaves your body. Feel the rise and fall of your chest or the sensation of air flowing through your nostrils. If your mind starts to wander (which it will!), gently bring your focus back to your breath without judgment.

Notice the Present Moment: After settling into your breath, start to notice what is happening in the present moment. What sounds do you hear around you? What sensations do you feel in your body? Are there any emotions or thoughts floating by? Observe everything with a sense of curiosity, but don't get attached to anything.

Stay Nonjudgmental: During these five minutes, let go of any need to label your thoughts as good or bad. If a stressful thought comes up, notice it and allow it to pass. Remember, you're not trying to stop your thoughts; you're practicing observing them without judgment. This is the key to being fully present.

Gently Come Back: After five minutes, slowly open your eyes and take note of how you feel. Do you notice a shift in your awareness or mood? How did your body feel during the exercise? Take a moment to reflect on the experience before you move on with your day.

Questions for Reflection

- How often do you find yourself either worrying about the future or dwelling on the past? What impact does this have on your sense of peace and happiness?

- Can you think of a recent moment where you were physically present but mentally absent? How might your experience have changed if you had been fully engaged in the present?

- What stories or thought patterns frequently pull you out of the present moment? How can you begin to recognize and let go of them?

- In what ways do you resist accepting the present as it is? How might embracing the present, even when it's uncomfortable, bring more peace into your life?

- What small practices can you incorporate into your daily routine to help ground you in the present moment?

- What are the simple pleasures in your life—like a meal, a

conversation, or a walk—that you tend to rush through? How can you slow down and savor them?

Conclusion

Living fully in the present is the key to unlocking peace and happiness in your life. The only moment you truly have is right now. When you make the choice to be present, you tap into a wellspring of joy, clarity, and contentment that's always available to you—no matter what's happening around you. So, start today. Slow down, breathe, and notice the richness of the moment you're in. It's where life is happening.

Final Reflection

The present moment is your greatest teacher, always offering lessons in stillness, acceptance, and gratitude.

6
Change Your Thinking to Live a Happier and Fuller Life

We all want to live a happy and fulfilled life, but what if the key to doing that lies not in changing our external circumstances, but in changing the way we think? The truth is, most of our stress, frustration, and unhappiness come not from the world around us, but from the stories we tell ourselves about it. The way we interpret life's events can either make us miserable or help us stay calm and content, no matter what's happening.

Think about it. Two people can experience the exact same situation—say, losing a job or going through a breakup—and come out of it with completely different mindsets. One might spiral into despair, while the other sees it as an opportunity for growth. The difference? How they think about it.

By learning to identify and challenge the negative thought patterns that hold you back, you can shift your perspective and start experiencing life in a whole new way. You can stop sweating the small stuff, let go of unnecessary worries, and create space for joy, peace, and fulfillment. The goal is to train your mind to work for you, not against you.

The Power of Thoughts: How They Shape Your Reality

Let's break this down a bit. Your thoughts have an enormous impact on how you feel and how you experience the world. If you constantly think, "I'm not good enough," or "Nothing ever works out for me," your brain believes it. Those negative thoughts trigger emotions like anxiety, sadness, or frustration, which then affect your behavior. You might avoid opportunities, lash out at others, or stay stuck in situations you don't like—all because your thoughts are feeding a false narrative.

On the flip side, when you consciously choose more positive, realistic thoughts, your brain starts to see things differently. You feel more confident, hopeful, and motivated. You take action, make better decisions, and create a cycle of positive momentum in your life. It's not magic; it's the power of perspective.

The good news is that you don't have to be at the mercy of your thoughts. You can learn to reshape them, question their validity, and replace them with more helpful, constructive ones. This is the key to living a happier, fuller life—one where you're in control of your mindset, rather than letting your mindset control you.

You don't have to be at the mercy of your thoughts.

Identifying and Challenging Negative Thoughts

The first step in changing your thinking is to become aware of the negative thoughts that are running the show. Often, we don't even realize we're thinking them because they've become automatic. It's like having a radio playing in the background all day—you don't always notice it, but it's influencing your mood.

Start paying attention to your thoughts, especially when you're feeling down, stressed, or anxious. What are you telling yourself in those moments? Common examples might be:

- "I'll never be good enough."
- "This is a disaster."
- "I can't handle this."

- "Why does this always happen to me?"

Once you've identified the negative thought, challenge it. Ask yourself:

- Is this thought based on facts, or is it just my perception?

- Am I catastrophizing or blowing this out of proportion?

- What's a more realistic or positive way to look at this situation?

For example, let's say you make a mistake at work and immediately think, "I'm such an idiot. I always mess things up." Instead of letting that thought take over, pause and challenge it. Is it really true that you always mess things up? Or is this just one mistake in an otherwise competent track record? A more balanced thought might be, "I made a mistake, but I've done well in the past, and I can fix this." Notice how that shifts your perspective from self-blame to problem-solving.

Reframing Your Perspective

Once you get the hang of identifying and challenging negative thoughts, the next step is to reframe them. This means taking a situation and intentionally choosing to view it from a more constructive or empowering angle.

Imagine you're facing a tough situation, like getting passed over for a promotion at work. The negative thought might be, "I'm never going to get ahead. What's the point in trying?" Instead, you could reframe it as, "This is disappointing, but it's an opportunity to reflect on what I can improve. I'll take this as a learning experience and keep pushing forward."

Reframing is not pretending everything is perfect or ignoring problems. It's choosing a mindset that helps you move forward instead of getting stuck. Life is full of challenges, but how you interpret them determines whether you grow from them or let them drag you down.

Letting Go of Irrational Demands

One of the main reasons we suffer unnecessarily is because we impose irrational demands on ourselves, others, and the world. We think, "I must succeed," or "People have to treat me fairly all the time," or "Things should go the way I want them to." But the reality is, life doesn't work that way. People aren't perfect, plans fall apart, and things rarely go exactly as we expect.

When we cling to these demands, we set ourselves up for frustration and disappointment. But when we let go of them and accept that life is unpredictable, we free ourselves from that mental strain. Instead of demanding that things be a certain way, we can adopt a mindset of acceptance and flexibility. This doesn't mean you stop striving for success or let people walk all over you—it just means you stop basing your happiness on things being perfect.

Start noticing where you have rigid expectations or demands in your life. Are you expecting perfection from yourself or others? Are you insisting that life follows your plan? Try loosening your grip and allowing things to unfold as they will. You'll be amazed at how much peace this simple shift can bring.

Practical Exercises to Shift Your Thinking

Here are some exercises to help you start changing your thought patterns and adopt a mindset that supports your happiness and well-being.

Daily Thought Awareness

Each day, take 5-10 minutes to write down your thoughts. Notice if any negative patterns emerge, such as self-criticism, catastrophizing, or overgeneralizing. Pick one thought and challenge it using the questions from earlier. Is it based on facts? Is there a more balanced way to think about it?

Reframe One Situation a Day

Pick one situation each day where you notice yourself feeling frustrated, upset, or anxious. Ask yourself, "How can I reframe this to see it from a more constructive perspective?" Write down both the negative interpretation and the reframe. For example, imagine you and your partner have a disagreement about something small, like forgetting to take out the trash. Your first thought might be, "They never listen to me. I'm always the one doing everything, and it's so frustrating." How could you reframe it? Instead of staying stuck in the negative, you could think, "We both have busy schedules, and sometimes things slip through the cracks. It's not about forgetting—it's about how we support each other moving forward. I can calmly remind them, and we'll tackle this together." By reframing, you focus on collaboration and understanding, rather than resentment. This simple shift can transform conflicts into opportunities for growth and better communication in the relationship. Over time, this will help train your brain to automatically look for the positive or growth-oriented side of things.

Release Your Irrational Demands

Identify one area in your life where you're holding onto an unrealistic demand (e.g., "I must be perfect"). Write down the demand, and then ask yourself, "Is this really true? What would happen if I let this go?" Try replacing the demand with a more flexible statement, such as "I'll do my best, but I don't need to be perfect to be happy" or "I can't control how others behave, but I can control how I respond."

▶ Immediate Action: Flip the Script on Negative Thoughts

This exercise is about identifying and replacing negative thought patterns with more empowering alternatives. You can implement it immediately to start shifting your thinking toward a happier and fuller life.

Steps:

Identify a Recurring Negative Thought: Think of one negative thought or belief that tends to pop up frequently in your life. This could be something like "I'm not good enough," "I always fail," or "People don't appreciate me."

Examine the Thought: Take a moment to ask yourself some key questions:

- Is this thought 100% true?
- What evidence do I have to support or challenge this thought?
- What's a more balanced or realistic way to think about this?

Flip the Script: Now that you've examined the thought, rewrite it in a more positive or constructive way. For example:

- Instead of "I'm not good enough," flip it to "I'm learning and growing every day, and I'm capable of improvement."
- Instead of "I always fail," flip it to "Even if I make mistakes, I learn from them and get stronger."
- Instead of "People don't appreciate me," flip it to "I choose to value myself, and I know the right people will see my worth."

Create a Positive Affirmation: Turn your reframe into a daily affirmation. Write it down somewhere visible, and repeat it to yourself every morning to reinforce the new belief. For example: "I am capable, I am growing, and I am enough."

This exercise is a powerful way to start retraining your brain to focus on possibilities instead of limitations. Over time, your new thought patterns will become second nature, helping you live with more joy and resilience. Whenever a negative thought arises, remind yourself to "flip the script" and seek out the empowering narrative. The more you practice this, the more your thinking will align with the life you want to create—full of happiness, fulfillment, and self-compassion.

Questions for Reflection

- What are the common negative thought patterns that you've noticed in your life? How do they affect your emotions, actions, and overall happiness?
- Can you recall a time when you interpreted a challenging situation in a negative light? How might reframing that situation

have changed your experience?

- Are there any irrational demands you place on yourself, others, or life in general? How could letting go of these demands bring more peace and flexibility into your life?

- How often do you take the time to challenge your thoughts? What specific strategies can you use to shift from negative thinking to a more constructive perspective?

- In what areas of your life are you clinging to expectations or rigid beliefs? How could adopting a more fluid mindset help you feel less frustrated or stressed?

- What daily habits can you develop to become more aware of your thoughts and practice reframing them for a happier, fuller life?

Conclusion

The more you train your mind to challenge negative thoughts, reframe situations, and let go of irrational demands, the more peace and happiness you'll find. Life won't always go your way, but by changing the way you think about it, you can live with more joy, resilience, and fulfillment. Remember, your thoughts create your reality, so why not choose thoughts that help you thrive?

Final Reflection

The thoughts you choose to nurture shape the reality you live in.

7

Identifying and Eliminating Self-Destructive Thought Patterns

We've all been there—stuck in our heads, replaying the same negative thoughts over and over. It's almost like our mind is on autopilot, dragging us down paths of self-doubt, worry, guilt, or frustration. But here's the truth: most of these thoughts are habits. And just like any habit, they can be changed.

The problem is, we often don't even realize we're caught in these negative loops. They feel so normal, so ingrained, that we mistake them for reality. But they're not. They're just stories we tell ourselves. The key to living a happier, more fulfilled life is recognizing those self-destructive thought patterns and learning how to break free from them.

So, how do you do that? It starts with becoming aware of these patterns, challenging them, and replacing them with healthier ways of thinking. Once you start identifying these negative thought habits, though, you'll be amazed at how much lighter and more in control of your life you feel.

Why We Get Stuck in Negative Thought Loops

Before we dive into how to fix this, let's talk about why we get stuck in these self-destructive thinking patterns in the first place. A lot of it comes down to conditioning. From a young age, we're taught certain beliefs about ourselves and the world. Some of those beliefs are helpful—like "be kind" or "work hard." But others can be harmful, especially when they lead us to doubt ourselves or feel like we're not enough.

Society, parents, teachers, friends—they all have their own sets of expectations, and we absorb those. Over time, we develop mental habits like guilt, fear of failure, or constant worry. These become so automatic that we don't even notice them anymore. They turn into self-imposed limitations, and we end up creating obstacles that don't need to be there.

The good news is, these are just patterns. And like any pattern, they can be broken.

Common Self-Destructive Thought Patterns

To start making a change, you first need to recognize the negative patterns that might be sabotaging your happiness. Here are some of the most common ones:

Perfectionism

This is the belief that if you're not perfect, you're somehow not good enough. It shows up as constantly striving for more, never being satisfied with what you've achieved, and beating yourself up over the smallest mistakes. Perfectionism is exhausting and unattainable. No one is perfect, and aiming for it will only leave you feeling disappointed.

Guilt and Regret

We all make mistakes, but holding onto guilt about the past is one of the fastest ways to keep yourself stuck. You can't change what's already happened, but you can learn from it and move forward. When you dwell on past mistakes, you're preventing yourself from enjoying the present and making the most of today.

Fear of Failure

Fear of failure is a big one. It keeps you from taking risks, trying new things, or stepping out of your comfort zone. The truth is, failure is a part of life, and it's how we learn and grow. If you're constantly afraid of failing, you're limiting yourself from all the amazing things you could accomplish.

Seeking Approval

This pattern shows up as needing constant validation from others. It means you're basing your self-worth on what other people think of you. The problem? You can't control other people's opinions. Seeking approval is a never-ending game, and you'll always feel like you're chasing after something you can't catch.

Negative Self-Talk

Ever catch yourself thinking, "I'm not good enough," "I'll never succeed," or "I don't deserve this"? That's negative self-talk. It's the little voice in your head that constantly criticizes and belittles you. The more you let it take over, the more you start to believe it—and those beliefs shape your reality.

> *If you're constantly afraid of failing, you're limiting yourself from all the amazing things you could accomplish.*

Catastrophizing

This is when you take a small issue and blow it way out of proportion. For example, if you make a mistake at work, you might think, "I'm going to get fired," even though the reality is, it's just a small bump in the road. Ask yourself, "Is this the worst thing that could happen, or am I overreacting? What's the most likely outcome here?"

All-or-Nothing Thinking

When you see things in extremes—either everything is perfect, or it's a total disaster. You might think, "If I don't do this perfectly, I'm a failure." Recognize that life isn't black and white. Look for the shades of grey. Ask yourself, "What's the middle ground here? What's another way to look at this?"

Overgeneralization

You take one negative event and assume it will happen again and again. For example, if you had one bad date, you might think, "I'm never going to find someone." One event doesn't define the future. Ask yourself, "Is there evidence that this always happens, or is this just one isolated incident?"

Personalization

When you take responsibility for things that are out of your control. For example, if someone is in a bad mood, you might think, "It's my fault, I must have done something wrong," even though their mood likely has nothing to do with you. Ask yourself, "Am I really responsible for this, or am I assuming blame that doesn't belong to me?"

How to Break Free from Self-Destructive Patterns

Now that you've identified some common thought patterns, let's talk about how to break them. The goal here is to replace those old habits with new, empowering ways of thinking. It's a process, but with practice, you can rewire your brain to think more positively and constructively.

Awareness is Key. As we already know, the first step in breaking any habit is becoming aware of it. Start by noticing when you're slipping into one of these patterns. When you feel stressed, anxious, or down, ask yourself: "What am I thinking right now? Is this thought helping me or hurting me?"

Simply becoming aware of the thought gives you power over it. You're no longer on autopilot.

Challenge the Thought. Once you've identified a negative thought, don't just accept it as truth. Question it! Ask yourself:

- Is this thought based on facts, or is it just my interpretation?
- Am I being too hard on myself?

- What would I say to a friend who was thinking this way?

By challenging the thought, you start to see it for what it is—just a thought, not reality.

Replace the Thought. After you've challenged the negative thought, it's time to replace it with something more constructive. For example:

- Instead of "I'm not good enough," try "I'm doing my best, and that's enough."
- Instead of "I'll never succeed," say "Success is a journey, and I'm making progress every day."

Reframing your thoughts takes practice, but the more you do it, the more automatic it becomes.

Let Go of Perfectionism. Perfection doesn't exist, so stop holding yourself to impossible standards. Instead of aiming for perfection, focus on progress. Celebrate your efforts and improvements, no matter how small. Remember, life is about growth, not flawlessness.

Stop Seeking Approval. You'll never be able to make everyone happy, so why waste your energy trying? Focus on approving of yourself. What matters most is how you feel about who you are and what you're doing. The more confident and self-assured you become, the less you'll need others' validation.

Practical Exercises to Eliminate Self-Destructive Thoughts

Daily Thought Journal

For the next week, keep a thought journal. Each day, write down any negative thoughts you notice—whether it's perfectionism, fear of failure, or seeking approval. Next to each thought, challenge it. Is it really true? What's a more balanced or positive way to think about it? This practice will help you become more aware of your thought patterns and give you the tools to change them.

Reframe Your Failures

Think of a recent failure or mistake. Instead of focusing on what went wrong, write down three things you learned from the experience. How did it help you grow? What can you do differently next time? This exercise will help you start seeing failure as a learning opportunity rather than something to be feared.

Self-Compassion Practice

Whenever you catch yourself being overly critical or harsh, pause and ask: "Would I speak to a friend this way?" Probably not. Treat yourself with the same kindness and understanding you would offer to someone you care about.Repeat this mantra: "I'm human, I'm doing my best, and that's enough."

Set Healthy Expectations

Identify one area of your life where you're holding yourself to unrealistic standards (e.g., work, relationships, body image). Write down what your current expectations are, then adjust them to be more realistic and compassionate. For example, if you expect yourself to be perfect at work, change that expectation to: "I will do my best at work, and it's okay if I make mistakes."

▸ Immediate Action: Uncover Your Root Beliefs

This exercise helps you dive deeper into your self-destructive thought patterns by identifying the core beliefs that drive them. Often, these limiting beliefs are buried beneath the surface and influence how you see yourself, others, and the world. By uncovering and challenging them, you can start breaking free from self-sabotage.

Steps:

Identify a Self-Destructive Thought: Start by picking one recurring negative or self-destructive thought, such as "I'll never be successful," "I don't deserve happiness," or "I always mess things up."

Dig Deeper – Ask Why: For each negative thought, ask yourself

"Why do I believe this?" Repeat this question several times to uncover the underlying root belief. For example:

"I always mess things up" → Why? → "Because I'm not capable enough" → Why? → "Because I've failed in the past and people have told me I wasn't good enough."

Challenge the Root Belief: Once you've identified the core belief, ask yourself:

- Is this belief true?

- Is this belief helpful? Does it push me forward or hold me back?

- What evidence do I have to challenge this belief? Can I think of times when I've succeeded or done well despite past failures?

Replace with a Healthier Belief: Now that you've identified and challenged the root belief, replace it with a more empowering one. For example:

"I always mess things up" → new belief → "I've made mistakes, but I've also succeeded many times. I'm capable of learning and improving."

Questions for Reflection

- Which self-destructive thought patterns do you recognize most in your own life? How have they impacted your decisions, relationships, or personal growth?

- When was the last time you caught yourself seeking external approval? How might your life change if you focused more on self-approval?

- How often do you find yourself engaging in perfectionism or fearing failure? What would happen if you embraced progress and imperfection instead?

- Can you identify a recent moment where you catastrophized or overgeneralized a situation? How could reframing it have led to a different emotional response?

- What unrealistic expectations are you holding onto, and how can you adjust them to be more compassionate toward yourself?

- What practical steps can you start taking today to challenge and replace the self-destructive thoughts that hold you back?

Conclusion: You Are in Control

The key takeaway here is that you have the power to change your thoughts. Self-destructive patterns don't define you—they're just habits your mind has picked up over time. By becoming aware of these patterns, challenging them, and replacing them with healthier ways of thinking, you can take control of your mindset and, ultimately, your life.

It's a process, but with practice, you'll find that the negative thoughts that once held you back start to lose their grip. You'll feel more empowered, confident, and free to live the life you want. So, start today. Pay attention to your thoughts, question them, and choose the ones that serve you. You've got this.

Final Reflection

Your mind can be both a prison and a key to freedom. With every thought, you have the power to shift the narrative and reclaim control over your life.

8

Be Kind to Yourself — The Power of Self-Compassion

Let's face it: life can be tough, and no one escapes the ups and downs. But what if I told you that the way you talk to yourself during those tough moments could make all the difference? Most of us are pretty good at being kind to others when they're struggling, offering a shoulder to cry on, or words of encouragement. But when it comes to ourselves, we tend to be our own worst critics. We beat ourselves up over every mistake, focus on our flaws, and expect perfection in everything we do. This relentless self-criticism can leave us feeling drained, anxious, and unworthy.

That's where self-compassion comes in. It's the simple but powerful idea that we should treat ourselves with the same kindness, care, and understanding that we would offer to a loved one. Think about it: when a friend messes up, do you call them names or tell them they're a failure? Of course not! You remind them that they're human, that everyone makes mistakes, and that they'll get through it. Self-compassion is about extending that same level of warmth and patience to yourself. And trust me, when you start being kind to yourself, life gets a lot lighter.

What Exactly Is Self-Compassion?

Self-compassion isn't a matter of giving yourself a free pass to slack off or never take responsibility for your actions or letting yourself off the hook. Instead, it's related to acknowledging that you're human, just like everyone else, and that imperfection is a normal part of life. It's about accepting your flaws and mistakes with an open heart and recognizing that you're worthy of love and kindness, especially in your hardest moments.

Self-compassion has three key components:

Self-Kindness

This is pretty straightforward: be kind to yourself. Instead of tearing yourself down when things don't go as planned, offer yourself words of comfort and understanding. Shifting from harsh self-judgment to self-nurturing.

Common Humanity

You're not alone in your struggles. Everyone goes through hard times, and everyone makes mistakes. Realizing that your suffering is part of the shared human experience helps you feel connected to others, rather than isolated in your pain.

> *We should treat ourselves with the same kindness, care and understanding that we would offer to a loved one.*

Mindfulness

Mindfulness is being present with your emotions without letting them overwhelm you. When something difficult happens, instead of drowning in self-pity or pushing your feelings away, mindfulness helps you recognize and sit with your emotions in a balanced way. You acknowledge your feelings without being consumed by them.

Why Self-Compassion Matters

If you've ever caught yourself in a cycle of self-criticism, you know how exhausting it can be. Criticizing yourself over and over doesn't make you stronger; it makes you feel defeated and stuck. On the other hand, self-compassion allows you to be human and make mistakes, and to grow from them without tearing yourself apart in the process.

People who practice self-compassion are more resilient. Why? Because they don't waste energy beating themselves up. They learn from their mistakes and move forward. They're also happier, less anxious, and have better relationships—both with themselves and others.

Think of self-compassion as a way to recharge your emotional battery. When you're kind to yourself, you're giving yourself the emotional support you need to keep going, even when things get tough.

How to Cultivate Self-Compassion

Now, you might be thinking, "This sounds great, but how do I actually start being kind to myself?" Well, like any new habit, it takes practice. But once you start, you'll find it gets easier and more natural over time. Here are some practical steps to help you develop self-compassion:

Notice Your Inner Critic

The first step is becoming aware of that critical voice inside your head. Pay attention to how you talk to yourself, especially when you're stressed, upset, or disappointed. Is your self-talk harsh or judgmental? Are you calling yourself names or making sweeping negative statements like, "I always mess up," or "Nobody likes me because I'm not interesting"?

Once you start noticing these patterns, you can begin to shift them. The next time you catch yourself being self-critical, pause and ask, "Would I say this to a friend in the same situation?" If the answer is no, then it's time to change the script.

Talk to Yourself Like a Friend

So yes, rather than being your harshest critic, try being your best friend. When you make a mistake, talk to yourself with the same kindness, patience, and understanding that you would offer to someone you care about. For example, if you didn't get that promotion you were hoping for, instead of saying, "I'm such a failure," you could say, "I'm disappointed, but I know I gave it my best shot. I'll learn from this and keep moving forward."

This shift in self-talk it's incredibly powerful. You'll start to feel more supported by yourself, which is a huge confidence booster.

Embrace Imperfection

By now I'm sure you know that perfection is an illusion. No one is perfect, and trying to be only sets you up for disappointment. Self-compassion is accepting that you're going to have bad days, make mistakes, and experience setbacks—and that's okay.

When you accept that imperfection is part of being human, you give yourself the freedom to learn and grow without the crushing pressure to be flawless. Remember, the goal isn't to be perfect; it's to be compassionate with yourself when you're not.

Practice Mindfulness

Mindfulness helps you stay present with your emotions without letting them take over. When you're going through a difficult time, it's easy to get caught up in negative emotions or try to push them away. But ignoring your feelings doesn't make them go away—it just buries them.

Rather, practice sitting with your emotions in a mindful way. Acknowledge how you feel without judgment. If you're upset, say to yourself, "I'm feeling sad right now, and that's okay." By recognizing your feelings without trying to change or suppress them, you create space for healing and growth.

Exercises for Building Self-Compassion

Let's get practical. Self-compassion is something you can actively cultivate in your daily life. Here are a few exercises to help you start being kinder to yourself:

Self-Compassion Break

The next time you're going through a tough moment, try taking a self-compassion break. Follow these steps:

- **Step 1**: **Acknowledge the difficulty**. Say to yourself, "This is a difficult moment," or "I'm having a hard time right now." This helps you recognize and validate your feelings.

- **Step 2**: **Remember you're not alone**. Remind yourself that everyone struggles at times. You could say, "Suffering is a part of life" or "I'm not alone in feeling this way."

- **Step 3**: **Be kind to yourself**. Offer yourself some words of kindness and encouragement. You might say, "May I be kind to myself" or "I'm doing the best I can." The key here is to offer yourself the same warmth and compassion you would give to a loved one.

Write Yourself a Compassionate Letter

Think of something you're struggling with right now. It could be a mistake you made, a disappointment, or a personal challenge. Now, imagine a close friend is going through the exact same thing. What would you say to them? How would you comfort and support them?

Write down those compassionate words—but address them to yourself. This exercise helps you tap into your natural ability to offer kindness and empathy and turn it inward.

Replace Self-Criticism with Self-Compassion

For the next week, pay attention to moments when you're critical of yourself. When you notice self-critical thoughts, stop and write them down. Then, rewrite each thought as a compassionate statement.

For example:

- Self-critical thought: "I'm so stupid, I can't believe I made that mistake."

- Self-compassionate response: "I made a mistake, but that's okay. I'm learning, and I'll do better next time."

Do this regularly, and you'll start to see a shift in how you relate to yourself.

Practice Gratitude Towards Yourself

We're often quick to appreciate others but rarely stop to appreciate ourselves. Take a moment each day to write down three things you appreciate about yourself. It could be something you accomplished, a kind gesture you made, or simply the fact that you're showing up and doing your best. This helps reinforce a positive, compassionate relationship with yourself.

▶ Immediate Action: Mirror of Compassion

This exercise encourages you to directly face yourself, both literally and figuratively, with kindness.

Steps:

Find a Quiet Space: Stand in front of a mirror in a quiet, undisturbed area. Look into your own eyes. At first, this might feel uncomfortable, but the key is to soften your gaze and observe yourself without judgment.

Acknowledge Your Struggles: Say aloud one thing that's been hard for you recently—whether it's a mistake, a disappointment, or a challenge. For example: "I've been really hard on myself about not meeting that deadline" or "I'm feeling overwhelmed by everything I need to do."

Speak Words of Kindness: Now, offer yourself some kind, compassionate words—just as you would to a close friend in the same situation. For example: "It's okay that I didn't meet the deadline. I'm doing the best I can, and that's enough" or "It's normal to feel overwhelmed. I'm human, and I deserve kindness, not criticism."

Repeat Daily: Do this practice each day, even if it's just for a few moments. Over time, this will help shift your inner dialogue toward kindness and support, helping you cultivate a habit of self-compassion in your everyday life.

Questions for Reflection

- How do you typically respond to yourself when you make a mistake or face a setback? Is your self-talk harsh, and how could you change it to be more compassionate?

- Think about a recent moment when you felt frustrated or disappointed. How could self-compassion have shifted your perspective in that situation?

- What does imperfection mean to you, and how might embracing your own imperfections bring you greater peace and self-acceptance?

- In what ways do you struggle with mindfulness when faced with negative emotions? How can you practice being more present with your feelings without being overwhelmed by them?

- What steps can you take today to start treating yourself with the same kindness and understanding that you offer to others?

- How might your life change if you let go of the need for perfection and embraced your humanity with compassion?

Conclusion: You Deserve Kindness

Learning to be kind to yourself is one of the most powerful things you can do for your mental and emotional well-being.

Self-compassion is about being human and recognizing that you're worthy of love and kindness, no matter what. So, the next time you find yourself in a tough spot, take a deep breath, give yourself a little grace, and remember—you deserve kindness, just like everyone else.

Final Reflection

In the quiet moments when you face your hardest challenges, remember: you are your own constant companion. How you choose to speak to yourself in those moments will shape not only your healing, but also the person you become.

II
Success and Productivity

Welcome to the section on Success and Productivity, where you'll uncover the strategies and mindset shifts that high achievers use to reach their goals and maximize their impact.

We'll explore the essential principles that fuel both personal success and financial independence. From igniting your inner drive to mastering productivity techniques, you'll learn how to harness the power of mindset, resilience, and belief. As you deepen your understanding of success strategies, you'll also discover the importance of financial education and how to balance material achievements with spiritual fulfillment. Prepare to unlock your full potential, work smarter, and create a life of abundance and purpose.

But first, take a moment to assess your current mindset, beliefs, and habits around success, productivity and financial independence. This assessment will help you identify areas where you're excelling and where you might need to focus more attention. Be honest with yourself and answer each question based on your first instinct.

Success and Productivity Self-Assessment

Check the box next to the response that best describes your current approach to success and productivity.

1. How would you rate your belief in your own ability to achieve success?

☐ A. I have an unshakeable belief that I can achieve anything I set my mind to.

☐ B. I believe I can succeed, but I often have doubts or let obstacles slow me down.

☐ C. I frequently question whether success is really possible for me.

2. How often do you take consistent action toward your goals?

☐ A. I take daily, consistent steps toward my goals, no matter the challenges.

☐ B. I take action, but I can be inconsistent or let setbacks stop me for a while.

☐ C. I struggle to take regular action and often find myself procrastinating.

3. How would you describe your attitude towards challenges and adversity?

☐ A. I see challenges as opportunities for growth and face them with resilience.

☐ B. I can deal with challenges, but I sometimes feel discouraged when things get tough.

☐ C. I tend to feel overwhelmed by challenges and struggle to stay motivated.

4. How do you approach financial education and managing your finances?

☐ A. I am actively educating myself about finances and have a solid plan for financial independence.

☐ B. I understand the basics of financial management, but I'm not always consistent in applying them.

☐ C. I don't prioritize financial education and feel unsure about how to manage my finances effectively.

5. When it comes to balancing material success and spiritual fulfillment, how do you feel?

☐ A. I've found a good balance between achieving material success and staying connected to my spiritual or inner values.

☐ B. I'm working on balancing both, but I often feel pulled more in one direction.

☐ C. I struggle to balance the two and often feel disconnected from my spiritual side when pursuing material goals.

6. How well do you manage your emotional state when striving for success?

☐ A. I'm skilled at managing my emotions and maintaining a positive attitude even in difficult times.

☐ B. I try to stay positive, but I'm easily affected by stress, fear, or self-doubt.

☐ C. My emotions often get the best of me, and I struggle to maintain a positive mindset.

7. How effective are you at identifying and focusing on the tasks that truly matter?

☐ A. I'm great at pinpointing them, and I focus most of my energy there.

☐ B. I have an idea of what my most important tasks are, but I'm often distracted by less impactful work.

☐ C. I find it hard to prioritize and often spend my time on tasks that don't move me forward much.

8. How much control do you feel you have over your mindset and personal growth?

☐ A. I feel empowered to change my mindset and harness universal energy to fuel my growth.

☐ B. I believe in the power of mindset, but I sometimes struggle to maintain a growth-oriented perspective.

☐ C. I often feel stuck and unsure how to shift my mindset toward personal growth.

Reflection & Next Steps

Mostly A's: You have a solid understanding of success principles and productivity strategies. The upcoming chapters will help you deepen your approach, refine your methods, and push your achievements to the next level, both personally and financially.

Mostly B's: You're on the right path, but there are areas where you can improve your focus and consistency. The next chapters will guide you in strengthening your mindset, building resilience, and mastering the balance between success and fulfillment.

Mostly C's: You may feel some uncertainty about how to achieve success and manage your growth. The following chapters will provide you with the tools and strategies to shift your mindset, focus your efforts, and unlock your full potential, both in your personal life and your financial journey.

9

Ignite Your Burning Desire and Unshakeable Belief

Let's talk about success. We all want it, right? Whether it's in your career, relationships, personal growth, or finances, success is something we all chase. But here's the thing: it doesn't just fall into your lap because you want it or because you're "lucky." The foundation of success is built on two powerful things: a burning desire and unshakeable belief in yourself. Without these, it's like trying to build a house without bricks. You might have the blueprints (the plan), but without the actual material (desire and belief), nothing happens.

Let's see how to turn that flicker of hope inside of you into a blazing fire that drives you forward, no matter what obstacles you face. We'll also talk about how to cultivate an unshakable belief in yourself—because without that inner confidence, even the strongest desire can fizzle out. Ready to unlock your potential and move towards success? Let's dive in.

What Is a Burning Desire?

A burning desire is more than just wanting something. It's an intense, almost obsessive focus on achieving your goal. It's the thing that gets you up in the morning, keeps you working late into the night, and pushes you through even the toughest setbacks. Imagine it like a fire inside of you—something that's always smoldering, and with the right fuel, it blazes hotter and stronger.

Think about it: whenever you really, really want something, you find a way to make it happen. Remember a time when you had a goal that you were determined to achieve? Maybe it was landing a job, finishing a degree, or saving up for something special. That drive you felt, that sense of purpose—it's what a burning desire is all about.

But it's not enough to just want something. You need to turn that want into a burning desire. The kind of desire that makes you feel like success is the only possible outcome.

How to Turn a Wish Into a Burning Desire

Most of us have vague wishes about what we want in life. "I want more money." "I want to be happy." "I want to start my own business." These are all nice ideas, but they lack the intensity to push you to act. A wish is passive—it's something you hope will happen. A burning desire, on the other hand, compels you to take action. It lights a fire under you to start doing, instead of just dreaming.

Here's how you turn a wish into a burning desire:

1. Get Crystal Clear About What You Want

A vague wish won't cut it. You need to know exactly what you want. Instead of saying, "I want more money," figure out exactly how much. Do you want to make $100,000 a year? Or do you want to have a million dollars in your bank account? The clearer your goal, the more powerful your desire becomes because you know exactly what you're working toward.

2. Know Why You Want It

This is huge. Why do you want this goal? What will achieving it do for you? Maybe earning more money means providing a better life for your family, traveling the world, or finally living debt-free. When you connect your goal to something that deeply matters to you, it transforms from a casual wish into something you need to achieve. Your "why" becomes the fuel that feeds your desire.

3. Visualize Your Success Every Day

Visualization is a tool that high achievers swear by, and it's because it works. Take a few minutes every day to close your eyes and imagine yourself achieving your goal. What does your life look like? How do you feel? Who's there with you? The more vividly you can imagine your success, the more real it becomes in your mind—and that strengthens your burning desire.

4. Turn Obstacles Into Opportunities

You will face obstacles. That's a fact. But instead of seeing these as reasons to quit, view them as part of the journey. The bigger the challenge, the bigger the reward when you overcome it. People with burning desire see setbacks as temporary and use them as stepping stones to success.

Belief in Yourself: The Secret Sauce

Now, let's talk about belief. Without belief in yourself, even the strongest desire won't get you far. Imagine having a burning desire to start a business, but every time you think about it, your mind says, "Who am I kidding? I'll never pull this off." That doubt is like pouring water on your fire—it extinguishes your motivation and kills your momentum.

Belief is what keeps that fire going strong, even when the odds are stacked against you. When you believe in yourself, you approach your goals with a sense of certainty. You know, deep down, that you can and will achieve what you set out to do.

How to Strengthen Your Belief in Yourself

If your self-belief is shaky right now, don't worry. Like any muscle, belief can be strengthened with practice. Here's how you can start building unshakable belief in yourself:

Affirmations. Affirmations are positive statements that help rewire your brain to focus on what's possible, rather than what's holding you back. If you keep telling yourself, "I'm not good enough," guess what? You'll believe it. But if you start affirming, "I am capable of achieving my goals," you'll begin to believe that too. Repeat affirmations daily, especially when doubt creeps in.

Some powerful affirmations you can use:

- "I am worthy of success."

- "I have everything I need to achieve my dreams."
- "I am confident in my abilities."

> *You know, deep down, that you can and will achieve what you set out to do.*

Remember Your Wins. Think back to times when you succeeded in something, even if it was small. Maybe you passed a difficult exam, learned a new skill, or got a promotion. These moments prove that you can succeed, and they serve as evidence that you have what it takes. When doubt hits, remind yourself of these wins to boost your confidence.

Act Like You Already Believe. This might sound strange, but sometimes you need to "fake it till you make it." Even if you don't fully believe in yourself yet, act as if you do. Make decisions, take actions, and approach challenges like someone who is confident in their success. Over time, your actions will build genuine belief.

Surround Yourself with Positive Influence. The people you spend time with have a huge impact on your mindset. If you're constantly around people who doubt you, or worse, criticize your dreams, it will wear you down. Surround yourself with positive, supportive people who believe in your potential. Their belief in you will help strengthen your own.

Combining Desire and Belief: The Magic Formula

Here's where things get exciting. When you combine a burning desire with unshakeable belief, you create a powerful formula for success. Desire pushes you to take action, while belief keeps you going when things get tough. Together, they create unstoppable momentum.

But remember: it's not just about thinking positive thoughts and waiting for things to happen. You need to back up your desire and belief with consistent action. Desire and belief are the fuel, but action is the vehicle that moves you towards your goal.

Practical Exercises to Ignite Your Desire and Belief

Let's make this real. Here are a few exercises you can start doing today to strengthen your desire and belief, and set yourself up for success:

Define Your Burning Desire

Grab a notebook and write down exactly what you want to achieve. Be specific. How much money do you want to make? What kind of lifestyle do you want? What kind of person do you want to become? The clearer you are, the better.

Next, write down why this goal matters to you. Dig deep. What will achieving this goal bring into your life? How will it improve your well-being, relationships, or career?

Visualize Your Success

Take 5-10 minutes every day to visualize yourself achieving your goal. Find a quiet space, close your eyes, and immerse yourself in the experience. Picture every detail of your success—what you're wearing, where you are, who's with you. Feel the emotions of joy and accomplishment. This simple exercise trains your mind to believe in your goal.

Affirmations for Belief

Pick 2-3 affirmations that resonate with you and start repeating them every day. You can write them on sticky notes and place them around your home, or say them out loud while looking in the mirror. The more you affirm your belief, the more natural it will feel.

Act Now

Take one small action today towards your goal. It doesn't have to be big, but it needs to move you forward. Maybe it's researching a course you want to take, emailing someone for advice, or saving $20 towards your financial goal. Action builds momentum, and momentum fuels belief.

▶ Immediate Action: Create a Vision Board for Your Goal

To harness your burning desire and unshakeable belief, take the time to visualize what success looks like for you. Creating a vision board is a powerful exercise that can keep you inspired and focused on your goals.

Steps to Create Your Vision Board:

Gather Your Materials: You'll need a large piece of poster board or a corkboard, scissors, glue, magazines, printouts, or any images and quotes that resonate with your goals.

Define Your Goals: Before you start cutting and pasting, spend a few minutes writing down your primary goals. Consider all areas of your life, including personal, professional, health, and relationships. Be specific about what you want to achieve.

Collect Images and Words: Go through magazines or search online for images, quotes, or words that represent your goals and dreams. Cut out or print these and keep them nearby.

Arrange and Create: Start placing the images and words on your board in a way that feels visually appealing to you. There's no right or wrong way to do this—just let your creativity flow! Consider grouping related goals or themes together.

Display Your Vision Board: Once your board is complete, find a prominent place to display it where you'll see it every day. This could be your office, bedroom, or even as the wallpaper on your phone.

Daily Reflection: Each morning, take a few moments to look at your vision board. Reflect on how you can take one small action towards each of the goals you've depicted. Allow the images and words to fuel your motivation and belief in your potential.

Questions for Reflection

- How strong is your current desire to achieve your goals? Is it a passing wish, or have you turned it into a burning desire that compels you to take action?

- What is your "why"? How does connecting your goals to a deeper purpose fuel your drive to succeed, especially when challenges arise?

- How often do you visualize your success? Are you able to clearly imagine what your life will look and feel like when you achieve your goals?

- Do you truly believe in your ability to succeed? If self-doubt creeps in, what steps can you take to start strengthening your belief in yourself?

- Think of a past success, big or small. How can reflecting on this achievement remind you of your capabilities and build confidence for future goals?

- What small action can you take today to build momentum towards your goal, and how will that action strengthen both your belief and desire?

Conclusion: You've Got This!

Desire and belief are the foundation of success. When you have a clear, burning desire and the unshakable belief that you can achieve it, you become unstoppable. It's not always going to be easy, but with these two forces working together, you have everything you need to reach your goals.

The fire within you is already there—now it's your turn to keep it burning.

Final Reflection

When you ignite your desire and build an unshakable belief in yourself, the obstacles ahead become stepping stones, not roadblocks.

10

The Secret Formula for Success—Talent, Effort, and Opportunity

Success is one of those things that everyone wants but few people really understand. We often look at someone who's made it big and think, "Wow, they must be incredibly talented," or, "They just got lucky." But the truth is that success isn't just about being gifted or catching a lucky break. In addition to the ingredient we have just covered in the previous chapter, success is a combination of three powerful ingredients: talent, effort, and favorable circumstances. When these elements come together in the right way, success becomes almost inevitable.

In this chapter, we're going to break down each of these ingredients and how they work together to create success. You'll see that while talent is important, it's not the be-all and end-all. Effort matters even more. And sometimes, the right opportunities—or what you might call "circumstances"—can be the final piece of the puzzle. By understanding this formula, you can start applying it to your own life to maximize your chances of success.

Ingredient 1: Talent—The Spark That Lights the Fire

Let's start with talent. Yes, natural talent does play a role in success. Some people are born with a knack for certain things, whether it's music, athletics, or math. Talent gives you a head start, a slight edge that makes learning and mastering a skill easier. But here's the catch: talent alone won't get you far.

Think of talent like a spark—it's helpful, but without something to ignite, it fades out. You could be the most naturally gifted writer, but if you never put pen to paper, your talent is wasted. So while talent is an important part of the equation, it's only the beginning.

Finding your natural strengths can feel like a daunting task, especially if you've never really thought about it. But here's the thing: we all have unique talents. Sometimes, they're just buried under layers of self-doubt or societal expectations. The key is learning how to recognize them.

Start by paying attention to the activities or tasks that come naturally to you. These are often the things you don't have to work hard at—they just flow. Maybe you've always had a talent for public speaking, or maybe you can solve complex problems with ease. Perhaps you have a great sense of humor and can lighten the mood in any room, or you're incredibly organized and can juggle multiple tasks effortlessly. These are clues pointing to your strengths.

Another way to uncover your talents is to reflect on the activities that make you feel energized. When you're doing something that aligns with your natural abilities, you often feel a sense of flow—time seems to fly by, and you're completely immersed in the task. Ask yourself: what activities do I find energizing or fulfilling, even if they require effort? Those are likely tied to your natural talents.

Ask for Feedback

Sometimes, it's hard to recognize our own strengths because we're so used to them—they feel "normal." This is where the perspective of others can be invaluable. Ask friends, family, or coworkers what they think you're naturally good at. You might be surprised by what they say.

Think about compliments you've received in the past. Have people often told you that you're a great listener, or that you have a knack for explaining things clearly? The strengths others see in you are often clues to talents you might overlook.

Look Back at Your Childhood

Your natural strengths often show up early in life, before social pressures and responsibilities take over. Take a trip down memory lane. What did you enjoy doing as a child? Were you the kid who loved organizing games for others, building things, or drawing for hours? These early interests can point to talents that may still be relevant, even if they've been neglected.

Explore Different Fields

If you're still unsure of your strengths, experiment! Try out new hobbies, take different classes, or volunteer in unfamiliar roles. By exposing yourself to a variety of experiences, you might discover hidden talents you never knew you had. For instance, you might try coding and realize you have a natural affinity for it, or take up photography and find a talent for visual storytelling.

> *What activities do I find energizing or fulfilling, even if they require effort?*

The more you experiment, the clearer your strengths will become.

Ingredient 2: Effort—The Fuel That Keeps the Fire Burning

Here's where most people misunderstand success: effort. Talent might give you a head start, but effort is what keeps you moving forward. You could be less naturally talented than someone else, but if you work harder, you can easily surpass them.

Effort is the long hours spent practicing, studying, refining, and improving. It's the grind, the persistence, and the resilience that carry you through the tough times. While talent gives you potential, effort turns that potential into real results.

The Power of the 10,000-Hour Rule

You've probably heard of the "10,000-hour rule," which says that to truly master something, you need to put in about 10,000 hours of practice. This rule highlights how essential effort is. No one becomes a master overnight. Even the most talented people in the world—whether it's athletes, musicians, or business leaders—have put in thousands of hours honing their craft.

Success is not about short bursts of energy; it's about consistent, long-term effort. When you combine effort with talent, you start to build momentum.

How to Build Consistent Effort:

- **Break It Down**: Big goals can feel overwhelming. Instead of focusing on the end result, break it down into smaller tasks. Want to write a novel? Start with writing one page a day. Want to run a marathon? Begin with a short jog around the block.

- **Practice Daily**: Consistency beats intensity. Practicing for 30 minutes every day is often more effective than a once-a-week, four-hour grind session. Small, regular actions build habits, and habits lead to mastery.

- **Stay Resilient**: There will be setbacks. Maybe you'll fail a test or lose a competition, but resilience is key. Every failure is an opportunity to learn and improve. The difference between successful people and everyone else is that they get back up and try again.

Ingredient 3: Circumstances—The Right Time, Right Place Factor

This is the part that people often overlook when they talk about success: circumstances. Being in the right place at the right time can make a huge difference. No matter how talented or hardworking you are, sometimes you just need that perfect opportunity to show what you've got.

Take the example of tech entrepreneurs like Bill Gates or Steve Jobs. Sure, they were talented and worked hard, but they also grew up during the rise of the personal computer industry. If they'd been born 50 years earlier or later, their success stories might have looked very different.

That's what we mean by circumstances—sometimes, the opportunities around you make all the difference. But before you throw your hands up and say, "Well, it's all luck then!"—there's good news. You can create your own favorable circumstances by staying prepared, seeking out opportunities, and recognizing them when they come.

How to Leverage Circumstances:

- **Stay Ready**: You never know when an opportunity might come knocking. Whether it's a chance meeting with someone influential, or a random job opening, you want to be prepared to seize it. Keep honing your skills so that when the right moment comes, you're ready to jump on it.

- **Seek Opportunities**: Don't wait for the perfect opportunity to fall into your lap. Actively search for ways to put yourself in favorable circumstances. Go to events, meet new people, explore different avenues. The more places you put yourself in, the more likely you are to find that "right time, right place" moment.

- **Say Yes**: Sometimes opportunities don't come wrapped in a neat package. They might come in the form of a project you didn't expect to be offered, or a challenge you weren't sure you wanted to take on. Be open to saying yes, even when something scares you or seems out of your comfort zone.

Bringing It All Together: The Success Formula

So, now that we've broken down the three key ingredients—talent, effort, and circumstances—let's bring them together. Success happens when these elements align.

Talent gives you the raw material to work with.

Effort shapes and refines that material into something meaningful.

Circumstances provide the opportunities to showcase your talent and effort in a way that leads to real success.

But here's the catch: you can't control everything. You can't decide what talents you're born with, and you can't always control the circumstances around you. What you can control is your effort and how you respond to the opportunities and challenges life throws your way.

Success isn't just about having one of these elements. It's about combining them all in the right way. Even if your talent is average, effort can take you far. And even if circumstances aren't perfect, with enough preparation and resilience, you can create your own luck.

Practical Exercises to Apply This Formula to Your Life

Identify Your Natural Talents

Take a moment to reflect on your natural strengths. What do people compliment you on? What do you pick up quickly? Make a list of these talents. If you're not sure, ask friends or family for feedback. Once you've identified your strengths, think about how you can develop them further. What's one small step you can take today to start working on your talent?

Create a 10,000-Hour Plan

Choose a skill or goal you want to master, and commit to a consistent practice routine. It doesn't have to be hours a day, but the key is consistency. For example, if you want to get better at writing, commit to writing 500 words a day. If you want to learn a new language, dedicate 20 minutes a day to practice. Create a timeline and stick to it.

Opportunity Hunting

Think about the field or area in which you want to succeed. What opportunities are available in that space? Are there events you could attend, people you could meet, or projects you could join? Make a list of five things you can do in the next month to actively put yourself in favorable circumstances.

Say Yes More Often

For the next week, challenge yourself to say "yes" to things you would normally shy away from. This could be accepting an invitation to a networking event, volunteering for a project at work, or trying something new that pushes you out of your comfort zone. The more you say yes, the more doors open.

▶ Immediate Action: Create an Opportunity Journal

To actively integrate the secret formula for success—talent, effort, and opportunity—into your life, start an Opportunity Journal. This exercise encourages you to remain aware of the opportunities around you and take actionable steps towards leveraging them for your success.

Steps to Create Your Opportunity Journal:

Set Up Your Journal: Use a notebook or digital platform where you can easily jot down your thoughts. Create sections for talent, effort, and opportunity.

Daily Reflection: At the end of each day, reflect on three questions:

- What opportunities did I encounter today? (e.g., conversations, networking events, learning moments)

- How did I apply my talents or skills to seize any opportunities?

- What effort did I put in to make the most of these opportunities?

Identify Opportunities: At least once a week, dedicate time to brainstorm new opportunities relevant to your goals. Consider:

- Networking events

- Workshops or seminars

- Online courses

- Community service projects

Plan Your Next Steps: For each opportunity you identify, write down at least one specific action you can take. This could involve reaching out to someone for a coffee chat, signing up for a workshop, or dedicating time to develop a skill that aligns with the opportunity.

Review and Adjust: At the end of each month, review your Opportunity Journal. Reflect on the progress you've made, the talents you've developed, and the efforts you've invested. Adjust your action steps as necessary based on what you've learned.

Questions for Reflection

- What are your natural talents, and how much effort have you put into developing them so far? Are there talents you've neglected because you've relied too much on natural ability?

- When was the last time you consistently committed to a long-term effort? How does your current level of effort align with the goals you want to achieve?

- Have you ever missed an opportunity because you weren't ready, or because you didn't recognize it? How can you better position yourself to take advantage of future opportunities?

- What circumstances in your life have contributed to your past successes? How can you actively seek out or create more favorable circumstances moving forward?

- Are you willing to say "yes" to opportunities outside your comfort zone, even when they don't seem perfect? How might stepping into the unknown open new doors for success?

- How do you balance talent, effort, and opportunity in your own life? Are there areas where you rely too much on one element and neglect the others?

Conclusion: The Path to Success is Yours to Build

At the end of the day, success isn't a mystery. It's the result of a blend of your talent, the effort you put in, and the circumstances you find—or create—for yourself. By focusing on what you can control (your effort and preparation) and staying open to opportunities, you'll set yourself on the path to achieving your goals.

Talent sparks the flame, effort keeps it burning, and circumstances fan it into a blaze. Combine all three, and you've got the formula for success—ready to be applied to your own journey.

Final Reflection

Success isn't a matter of luck or talent alone—it's a delicate dance between what you're given, what you're willing to work for, and the opportunities you create.

11
Unlock Your Potential with NLP

Have you ever wondered why some people seem to effortlessly achieve their goals, while others struggle despite putting in the same, or even more, effort? The answer isn't luck or talent. It's how you program your mind. And here's the kicker—you can take control of that programming, rewire your brain, and start achieving things you didn't think were possible.

That's where Neuro-Linguistic Programming (NLP) comes in. NLP is a set of techniques designed to help you change the way you think, communicate, and behave in order to achieve the results you want. It's recognizing that your thoughts and beliefs shape your reality, and by changing those, you can change your outcomes.

This chapter will walk you through the basics of how NLP works and show you some practical, easy-to-understand techniques that you can start using today to get closer to your goals. Whether you want to boost your confidence, improve your relationships, or finally achieve that big dream you've been working toward, NLP can help you get there.

What Is NLP, Really?

First, let's break it down:

Neuro refers to your brain and nervous system—how you think, feel, and perceive the world.

Linguistic is about language, both the words you use with others and the internal dialogue you have with yourself.

Programming is how you've been "wired" to act in certain ways based on past experiences, habits, and beliefs.

NLP is becoming aware of that wiring and then reprogramming your brain so you can live more intentionally. It's like updating the software on your phone to a new version that works better, faster, and gets you where you want to go.

The Power of Your Mind: How Beliefs Shape Your Reality

Let's start with the basics. Your mind is incredibly powerful, but here's the catch: it believes what you tell it. If you constantly tell yourself things like "I'm not good with numbers" or "I'll never achieve my goals," your mind takes that as truth, and you act in ways that align with those beliefs.

Think of your mind as a GPS. If you put in the wrong address, you're going to end up in the wrong place. In the same way, if your beliefs are negative or limiting, they'll steer you toward failure or frustration. But if you put in the right "address" by programming your mind with empowering beliefs, you'll head straight toward success.

What you believe about yourself directly affects your behavior, and your behavior shapes your results. If you believe you're capable, you'll act confidently, and you'll be more likely to succeed. If you believe you're doomed to fail, you'll hesitate, self-sabotage, or give up too soon.

What you believe about yourself directly affects your behavior, and your behavior shapes your results.

Reprogramming Your Mind: The NLP Toolbox

Now that we've got the basics down, let's get into the fun part: how to actually reprogram your brain using NLP techniques. These are practical, step-by-step strategies that help you shift your mindset and create the outcomes you want.

Anchoring: Create Positive Emotional Triggers

Have you ever noticed how a certain song can instantly make you feel happy or energized? That's because it's linked to a memory or emotion in your brain. Anchoring is the process of deliberately creating that link so you can trigger positive emotions on demand.

How to Use Anchoring:

- Choose a state you want to feel—confidence, calm, motivation, whatever works for your goals.

- Close your eyes and imagine a time when you felt that emotion strongly. Make the memory as vivid as possible: what did you see, hear, feel?

- As you feel the emotion build, create a physical anchor—this could be something like pressing your thumb and forefinger together, or clenching your fist.

- Repeat this a few times, each time associating the anchor with the positive emotion.

Once you've set the anchor, you can trigger that positive state whenever you need it by simply using your anchor (e.g., pressing your thumb and forefinger together) during moments when you need a confidence boost or want to feel calm before a big presentation.

Reframing: Change the Meaning, Change the Feeling

Reframing is all about changing the way you see a situation. In any challenging moment, you can choose to focus on the negative aspects, or you can look at it from a new, more empowering perspective.

Let's say you didn't get the promotion you wanted. Your initial thought might be: "I'm not good enough." But with reframing, you can shift that to: "This is an opportunity to grow and learn. I'm going to get even better at my job and show them my true value next time."

By changing the meaning of an event, you change how you feel about it—and that feeling influences your actions going forward.

How to Reframe:

- Identify a situation or belief that's causing you stress or frustration.

- Ask yourself: "What's another way to look at this? How can I turn this into a learning experience or opportunity?"

- Focus on the new meaning and let go of the old, negative interpretation.

The NLP Formula for Achieving Your Goals

One of the most powerful aspects of NLP is that it gives you a clear formula for achieving your goals. It's not just about hoping for the best or waiting for things to magically fall into place. It's about using specific strategies to create real, measurable results.

Set Clear, Specific Goals

NLP is all related to clarity. The more specific your goals, the easier it is for your brain to work toward them. Vague goals like "I want to be successful" don't give your mind a clear target to aim for. Instead, break it down: "I want to increase my income by 20% in the next six months by taking on new clients and improving my marketing skills."

Visualize Success

Your brain can't tell the difference between something real and something vividly imagined. So when you visualize yourself achieving your goals, your mind begins to treat it as reality, and you start acting in ways that bring that vision to life.

How to Visualize:

- Close your eyes and imagine yourself reaching your goal. Picture it in detail: what are you doing, what do you feel, what do you see around you?

- Make the visualization as vivid as possible. The more senses you involve (sight, sound, touch, etc.), the more effective it is.

- Do this regularly—daily, if possible—and let yourself fully experience the emotion of already having achieved what you're aiming for.

Take Action and Adjust

NLP emphasizes the importance of taking consistent action and adjusting your approach as needed. When you set a goal, you won't always know exactly how to get there, but by taking small steps, observing what works, and tweaking your approach, you'll keep moving forward.

Don't get stuck in "analysis paralysis" where you wait until everything is perfect before acting. Start where you are, and as you learn more, you can refine your strategy.

Practical Exercises to Apply NLP in Your Life

Now, let's make this actionable. Below are some exercises that will help you apply NLP principles and start reprogramming your mind for success.

Goal Mapping Exercise

- Write down one specific goal you want to achieve in the next three months.

- Break the goal down into smaller, actionable steps. What can you do today, this week, or this month to move closer to your goal?

- Create a mental image of yourself having already achieved this goal. Spend 5-10 minutes every day visualizing it as vividly as possible.

Anchor Your Confidence

- Think of a time when you felt incredibly confident or powerful.

- Replay that moment in your mind. As you feel the confidence build, create a physical anchor (e.g., placing your hand over your heart).

- Practice this daily so you can use your anchor anytime you need a boost of confidence.

Reframe a Challenge

- Think about a recent challenge or setback.

- Ask yourself: "What's another way I can look at this? How can this challenge serve me in the long run?"

- Write down the new, empowering interpretation and remind yourself of it whenever you think about that situation.

▶ Immediate Action: Swish Pattern for Breaking Limiting Habits

The Swish Pattern is a classic NLP technique that helps you replace negative or limiting habits with more empowering ones. You can use this to program your mind for success by breaking unhelpful behaviors and replacing them with positive ones.

Steps:

Identify a Limiting Behavior: Think of a habit or reaction you want to change (e.g., procrastination, self-doubt, or overreacting to stress).

Visualize the Old Behavior: Close your eyes and picture a scene where you're engaging in that limiting behavior. Make this image clear and vivid—see yourself doing the action, feel the emotions, and notice what happens in the scene.

Create a New Image of Success: Now, imagine how you want to behave instead. Create a positive image where you're acting in a more empowering way (e.g., staying calm under pressure, completing tasks with focus, or approaching challenges confidently). Make this image bright, detailed, and emotionally charged with the feelings of success and achievement.

Swish the Images:

- Hold both images in your mind: the old behavior (limiting) and the new one (empowering).

- Start with the limiting image large and close in your mind. Then, in an instant, "swish" the new empowering image into focus, making it bigger, brighter, and more powerful, while the old image fades away into the distance.

- Repeat this swish process quickly five to ten times, each time making the new image more vivid and the old one less significant.

Anchor the New Behavior: After completing the Swish pattern, open your eyes and imagine yourself encountering the situation in real life. Picture yourself immediately using the new, positive behavior. Repeat this process daily to reinforce the new pattern in your mind.

Questions for Reflection

- What are the limiting beliefs you've been telling yourself, and how have they shaped your actions and results?

- How can you reframe a recent setback to see it as an opportunity for growth?

- What emotional states do you want to trigger more easily in your life, and how can you use anchoring to achieve this?

- Are your goals specific and clear enough for your brain to act on? How can you break them down further into actionable steps?

- What small, consistent actions can you take today to move closer to your goals while being open to adjusting your approach?

- How do you currently visualize your success? Are your visualizations vivid enough to engage your emotions and senses fully?

Conclusion: The Power is in Your Hands

The beauty of NLP is that it puts the power back in your hands. You're not a victim of your circumstances or past programming—you have the ability to rewrite your story, change your beliefs, and create a life that aligns with your deepest goals and desires.

By using these techniques, you're not only shifting the way you think and feel, but you're also setting yourself up for long-term success. Whether it's anchoring positive emotions, reframing challenges, or visualizing your goals, NLP gives you the tools to unlock your full potential.

The key to achieving your goals is working smarter by using the most powerful tool you have—your mind.

Now it's your turn. Start practicing these techniques, and watch how your mindset—and your life—begins to shift!

Final Reflection

Your mind holds the keys to your future, and every belief, every thought, is part of a program that you have the power to rewrite.

12

The Science of Success: How to Apply Proven Principles to Achieve Greatness

Success often seems like an elusive concept but it isn't just some abstract idea, it is something that can be systematically approached. What if you could apply scientific principles to reach success in any area of life—whether in your career, relationships, health, or personal development?

Success is applying strategies that are rooted in scientific thinking, patterns of behavior, and cause-and-effect relationships. The truth is, there's a method to the madness, and once you know how to apply these proven principles, you can unlock the potential for success in ways you might never have thought possible.

So, let's break it down. Here's how to use scientific principles to create measurable, consistent success in your life.

Set Clear, Specific Goals

The first step in achieving success is knowing exactly what you're aiming for. As we talked before, most people have vague, undefined goals. "I want to be healthier," "I want to make more money," or "I want to be happier", aren't clear goals. They're desires. For goals to be effective, they need to be specific, measurable, and actionable.

Scientists rely on clear hypotheses to test, and your goals should work the same way. A specific goal helps you focus your efforts and gives you something concrete to measure your progress against. For example:

Instead of "I want to be healthier," set a goal like, "I want to lose 10 pounds in three months by working out three times a week and eating 1,800 calories a day."

Instead of "I want more money," say, "I want to earn $10,000 more this year by improving my skills and applying for a promotion."

Specific goals give you a direction, help you track progress, and allow you to adjust your actions along the way.

Exercise: Write down one specific, measurable goal for yourself in any area of life. Include a deadline, clear steps, and how you will measure success.

Focus on Cause and Effect

One of the most powerful ideas in science is the principle of cause and effect. Every outcome has a cause, and if you can identify the key factors that lead to success, you can replicate them. This means you need to be observant and analytical about what's working and what's not in your life.

Let's say you want to improve your productivity at work. If you notice that you're always less productive in the afternoon, ask yourself, "What's causing this dip?" Maybe it's your diet, maybe it's too many distractions, or maybe you're just burning out by lunch. By identifying the causes of low productivity, you can take action—whether that means taking short breaks, eating healthier, or organizing your tasks differently.

Apply this mindset to any area where you want to succeed. If you know what triggers good results, double down on those actions. If you notice patterns of failure or inefficiency, tweak or eliminate the behaviors that lead to them.

Exercise: Identify one area where you are struggling to achieve your goals. Analyze what might be causing those roadblocks. What actions, habits, or circumstances could be affecting your progress? Write down a few possible changes you can make to address these causes.

Use Feedback Loops

In science, experiments are repeated over and over to collect data and adjust methods for better results. Your journey to success should be no different. Feedback loops are essential for refining your approach. If something isn't working, don't just give up—adjust your method, take new actions, and try again.

Let's say you've set a goal to save $5,000 in six months, but after two months, you've only saved $500. What happened? Look at your spending habits and see where you went wrong. Did you splurge on non-essential items? Did unexpected expenses come up? Once you have this feedback, you can adjust your budget, cut back on unnecessary purchases, or find ways to increase your income.

The key here is to view failure as data. It's not a reflection of your worth or ability; it's just information. With each failure, you learn something new about what works and what doesn't. The more you refine your process, the closer you get to success.

Exercise: Think about a recent failure or setback. What went wrong, and why? Write down what you can learn from this and how you can adjust your actions going forward.

The Power of Incremental Progress

One of the biggest mistakes people make when trying to achieve success is expecting overnight results. In science, breakthroughs often come after many small experiments and incremental progress. The same applies to your personal journey. Success doesn't happen all at once. It's the result of consistent, small improvements over time.

For example, if your goal is to get fit, expecting to transform your body in a month is unrealistic. But, as we discussed in a previous chapter, if you focus on improving by 1% every day—whether it's lifting a little more weight, running a bit farther, or making slightly healthier choices with your food—those small improvements compound over time into massive progress.

Think about this: improving by just 1% every day means you'll be 37 times better by the end of the year. The power of small gains is extraordinary.

Exercise: Pick one area where you want to improve. Commit to making a 1% improvement every day for the next week. Track your progress and see how those small steps add up over time.

> *The key here is to view failure as data. It is not a reflection of your worth or ability; it is just information.*

Leverage the Power of Systems

In science, researchers use systems and repeatable processes to get consistent results. You can apply the same principle to your life by creating systems that support your success. A system is essentially a set of behaviors or routines that help you reach your goals without relying on constant willpower.

For instance, if you want to be more productive, create a morning routine that sets you up for success. Maybe it involves waking up at the same time, doing a bit of exercise, and tackling your most important task first. By creating a system that removes decision-making and guesswork, you increase your chances of sticking to productive habits.

Success isn't about working harder every day, is designing systems that make success inevitable.

Exercise: What systems do you currently have in place to support your goals? Identify one area where you can create or improve a system. For example, if you're trying to eat healthier, set up a weekly meal prep routine. Write down how you will design and implement this system.

Surround Yourself with the Right People

Scientists often work in teams or collaborate with others because success is rarely a solo effort. Surrounding yourself with the right people can amplify your chances of success. You become the average of the five people you spend the most time with, so if you're constantly around negative, unmotivated people, that will rub off on you.

On the other hand, if you surround yourself with driven, optimistic people who are working towards their goals, you'll naturally be more inclined to push yourself. These people will challenge you, support you, and provide valuable insights that can help you grow.

Exercise: Reflect on the people you spend the most time with. Are they helping you grow, or holding you back? Make a plan to spend more time with those who inspire and motivate you, and distance yourself from those who drain your energy or pull you away from your goals.

Applying the Scientific Method to Your Goals

Let's get practical with these steps to apply everything we have just learned:

Step 1: Define a Clear, Measurable Goal

Choose one specific goal from any area of your life—career, health, relationships, or personal development. This goal should be specific, measurable, and time-bound. Avoid vague goals like "I want to be healthier" or "I want to be more successful." Instead, think of something concrete you can track, such as:

- "I want to increase my monthly income by $2,000 within six months."

- "I want to lose 15 pounds in the next three months by exercising three times a week and following a meal plan."

Write down your goal, making sure it is both challenging and realistic. The clearer and more specific it is, the easier it will be to measure your progress.

Step 2: Identify the Key Causes for Success

Once you've defined your goal, think about the key factors (or "causes") that will lead to the outcome you want. These are the 1-3 most important actions you can take to drive progress towards your goal.

For example:

If your goal is to increase income, your key causes could be:

- Upskilling through relevant courses.
- Networking with industry professionals.
- Applying for new job opportunities or freelance gigs.

If your goal is to lose weight, your key causes might be:

- Following a consistent exercise routine.
- Maintaining a calorie deficit through a balanced diet.
- Getting 7-8 hours of sleep per night.

These key actions should be specific and within your control. Write them down.

Step 3: Create a System to Make Success Automatic

Systems are repeatable processes that help you stay consistent in your actions.

For your goal, design a system that will make it easier to follow through with your key actions. For example:

If your goal is to increase your income, set up a daily or weekly system for job applications or professional development. You could schedule 30 minutes each morning to search for new opportunities or practice new skills.

If your goal is to lose weight, create a system for meal prepping on Sundays and setting up a workout schedule for the week.

The goal is to make these actions part of your routine, so they require less effort to execute consistently.

Step 4: Track Your Progress and Adjust with Feedback

Finally, you need a way to measure progress and make adjustments based on what's working and what's not. This is your feedback loop. Just as scientists refine their experiments based on data, you should regularly review your results and tweak your approach.

Set up a system to track your progress. It could be:

- A journal where you record daily or weekly progress (e.g., tracking weight loss or income changes).

- A spreadsheet where you log actions, such as how many job applications you submitted or how many workouts you completed.

- An app that helps you monitor habits, calories, or other key metrics related to your goal.

Then, set a timeline for reviewing your progress (e.g., every week or every two weeks). During this review, ask yourself:

- What's working well?

- What's not working, and why?

- What adjustments can I make to improve my results going forward?

Make it a point to view setbacks as data, not failure. If something doesn't work as planned, it's simply an opportunity to refine your process and experiment with a new approach.

▸ Immediate Action: Conduct an Experiment

The scientific method is a systematic approach to solving problems through observation, experimentation, and adjustment. You can apply this principle to your life by treating your goals and challenges like a personal experiment.

Steps:

Define Your Hypothesis: Think about one goal or challenge you want to tackle. Instead of just hoping for success, frame it as a hypothesis. For example, "If I wake up one hour earlier every day, I will be more productive."

Conduct an Experiment: Now that you have a hypothesis, test it. Start implementing your idea consistently over a set period of time (e.g., one week or one month). Make sure to track your actions and results.

Analyze Your Results: After the set period, review your findings. Did waking up earlier actually make you more productive? What other factors influenced your results? Consider both the positive and negative outcomes. If the experiment didn't work out as expected, that's okay—this is all data.

Refine Your Approach: Based on your analysis, tweak your approach and try again. If waking up early didn't work, maybe you need a better evening routine to ensure you get enough rest. Keep adjusting until you find the right combination of actions that lead to success.

Repeat the Cycle: Continuously apply this process to different areas of your life. With each iteration, you'll become more precise and effective in pursuing your goals, just like a scientist fine-tuning an experiment.

Questions for Reflection

- Are your current goals clear, specific, and measurable? If not, how can you refine them to be more actionable?

- What patterns of cause and effect have you noticed in your life? How can you leverage those that lead to success and eliminate those that hinder progress?

- How do you currently react to failure or setbacks? Do you see them as data to learn from, or as personal shortcomings?

- What systems do you have in place to support your success? How can you improve or create new systems that make progress automatic?

- Who are the five people you spend the most time with, and how do they influence your mindset and actions? Do they inspire and motivate you, or do they hold you back?

- What is one small, 1% improvement you can make today in an area where you want to see growth?

Conclusion: Success is a Science You Can Master

Success is applying proven principles, adjusting your approach, and making steady progress over time. By setting clear goals, focusing on cause and effect, using feedback loops, and surrounding yourself with the right people, you can systematically work towards success in any area of life.

You don't have to guess your way to success. With the right mindset and the tools you now have, you can approach success like a scientist—experimenting, learning, and growing until you reach your goals.

Final Reflection

The science of success is about mastering the small, daily actions that compound over time.

13
Positive Attitude and Emotional Management for a Full Life

Imagine waking up each day feeling calm, optimistic, and ready to tackle whatever comes your way. Life may not always be easy, but you're equipped with a mindset and emotional toolkit that allows you to navigate its ups and downs with grace and resilience. That's the magic of mastering a positive attitude and emotional management—two of the most powerful forces that can transform your life for the better.

Let's break it down. We're constantly faced with situations that can trigger stress, frustration, or disappointment. But what if, instead of reacting automatically, you could choose how to respond? What if you had the ability to control how you feel, regardless of what happens around you? That's not wishful thinking—it's a skill you can develop.

In this chapter, we're going to explore how cultivating a positive attitude and managing your emotions are the keys to leading a fuller, happier life.

The Power of a Positive Attitude: Rewiring Your Mind

We've all heard the saying, "Look on the bright side." And while it might sound cliché, there's real science behind the benefits of maintaining a positive attitude. But don't confuse "positive thinking" with ignoring reality or pretending everything is perfect. It's about focusing on the opportunities, lessons, and solutions that arise from challenging situations rather than dwelling on the problems.

A positive attitude starts with how you interpret the world around you. Do you see obstacles as barriers or as challenges that help you grow? When things don't go your way, do you focus on what you've lost, or do you look for what you can learn? Shifting your mindset this way doesn't mean you'll never feel upset or stressed, but it helps you handle life's curveballs with more resilience and grace.

How to Cultivate a Positive Attitude:

- **Practice Gratitude**: A great way to cultivate positivity is by regularly practicing gratitude. Focusing on what you're thankful for—no matter how small—rewires your brain to notice the good things in your life. For example, instead of dwelling on the fact that you're stuck in traffic, you might appreciate having the time to listen to your favorite podcast. It's all about perspective.

- **Challenge Negative Thoughts**: When negative thoughts creep in, challenge them. Ask yourself, "Is this thought really true? Am I blowing this out of proportion?" Often, our minds tend to jump to worst-case scenarios, but by stopping to question those thoughts, we can see situations more objectively.

- **Surround Yourself with Positivity**: As we saw earlier, the people you spend time with influence your attitude. If you're around negative, complaining people all the time, their energy can rub off on you. Make an effort to surround yourself with positive, uplifting people who inspire you.

Emotional Management: Taking Control of How You Feel

Emotions are a normal part of being human. We experience a whole range of them every day, from happiness to frustration, excitement to sadness. But many people live at the mercy of their emotions, reacting impulsively when they're angry, stressed, or upset. The good news is that you can learn to manage your emotions instead of letting them manage you.

Emotional management doesn't mean suppressing your feelings or pretending everything is fine when it's not. It's about understanding and regulating your emotions in a way that helps you stay calm and in control, even in difficult situations.

Steps to Master Emotional Management:

- **Acknowledge Your Emotions**: The first step in managing

emotions is simply being aware of them. Often, we push down uncomfortable feelings, hoping they'll go away on their own. Instead, try acknowledging how you feel. "I'm feeling really anxious right now," or "I'm frustrated because this meeting didn't go as planned." Naming your emotions can help you understand and process them.

- **Pause Before Reacting**: When you feel a strong emotion rising, pause. Take a deep breath. This gives you a moment to choose how to respond, rather than reacting impulsively. For example, if someone says something that irritates you, instead of snapping back, take a moment to collect your thoughts and respond calmly.

- **Shift Your Focus**: If you're stuck in a negative emotional state, one of the best ways to shift out of it is to change your focus. Take a walk, listen to music, or talk to a friend. Focusing on something else for a while helps create emotional distance and allows you to come back to the situation with a clearer, calmer mind.

Learn to manage your emotions instead of letting them manage you.

How Positive Attitude and Emotional Management Work Together

When you combine a positive attitude with emotional management, you create a powerful synergy that helps you thrive in all areas of life. Here's why:

A positive attitude gives you the perspective that things will work out, even when life gets tough. It helps you focus on solutions instead of problems.

Emotional management gives you the tools to stay calm and focused when challenges arise. It helps you avoid impulsive reactions that can make a situation worse.

Together, these two skills create a feedback loop. The more you manage your emotions, the easier it becomes to maintain a positive attitude. And the more you cultivate positivity, the less likely you are to let negative emotions take over.

Real-Life Example:

Let's say you've been working hard for a promotion, but your boss gives it to someone else. Naturally, this situation might trigger feelings of frustration, disappointment, and maybe even anger.

Here's how combining a positive attitude and emotional management can help:

Pause and Acknowledge Your Emotions: Instead of letting your frustration take over, pause and recognize how you're feeling. You might say to yourself, "I'm really disappointed right now. I feel like all my hard work wasn't recognized."

Shift Your Focus: Instead of ruminating on what you lost, shift your focus. Maybe there's a lesson to be learned from this experience. You might think, "What can I do differently next time to stand out more?"

Adopt a Positive Perspective: Finally, take a positive view of the situation. Maybe this wasn't the right opportunity for you, and something even better is on the horizon. By focusing on what you can control and remaining optimistic about the future, you set yourself up for success in the long run.

Why Attitude and Emotional Management are the Keys to a Full Life

Ultimately, the way you think and manage your emotions determines the quality of your life. Here's why:

Your thoughts shape your reality. If you constantly expect the worst, you're more likely to experience negativity and disappointment. But if you approach life with an open, positive mindset, you're more likely to attract good things and handle challenges with resilience.

Your emotions drive your actions. When you're in control of your emotions, you make better decisions and respond to life's challenges with calm and clarity. But if you let emotions control you, your actions become reactive, and you're more likely to make impulsive choices that lead to regret.

By mastering these two areas, you can navigate life with greater confidence, resilience, and peace.

Practical Exercises for a Positive Attitude and Emotional Management

Now that you understand the importance of a positive attitude and emotional management, let's put this wisdom into practice with a few simple exercises.

Daily Gratitude Practice

Every day, write down three things you're grateful for. They don't have to be big things—they can be as simple as "I had a delicious breakfast," or "I enjoyed a walk in the park." Practicing gratitude regularly trains your brain to focus on the positive aspects of your life, which strengthens your overall mindset.

Emotional Check-In

Set a timer to go off three times a day. When it rings, stop for a moment and ask yourself, "How am I feeling right now?" Just acknowledging your emotions helps you become more aware of your internal state, which is the first step to managing it. Over time, you'll become better at recognizing your emotions and choosing how to respond.

Reframe Negative Thoughts

The next time you catch yourself thinking something negative, like "I always mess things up," or "Nothing ever goes right for me," pause and reframe it. Replace the thought with something more constructive, like "I'm learning from this mistake," or "I've overcome challenges before, and I can do it again."

▶ Immediate Action: Mood Shifting Through Music

Music is a powerful tool for emotional management, and it can be used to shift your mood and attitude almost instantly. By deliberately choosing music that aligns with the emotions you want to experience, you can take control of your emotional state in real-time. This exercise will help you create a playlist designed to elevate your mood, promote positivity, and manage emotions effectively.

The Mood-Boosting Playlist:

Identify Your Emotional Goals: Think about the emotions you want to cultivate on a daily basis—whether it's joy, calmness, motivation, or confidence. Write down 2-3 emotional states you'd like to enhance or strengthen in your life.

Select Music That Matches Those Emotions: For each emotional state, pick 3-5 songs that evoke those specific feelings. Choose songs that make you feel joyful, peaceful, or energized. Pay attention to how the music affects your body and mood as you listen.

Create Your Personalized Mood Playlist: Create a playlist with all these selected songs, categorizing them by emotion (e.g., "Calm," "Confidence," or "Happiness"). This playlist will become your emotional management tool, one you can turn to anytime you need a mood shift.

Use the Playlist Intentionally: When you find yourself in a negative emotional state or need a boost of positivity, play the appropriate songs from your playlist. Close your eyes, listen deeply, and let the music guide you into the desired emotional state.

Daily Listening Practice: Make a habit of listening to your playlist for at least 10 minutes each day. Whether it's during a morning routine, on a break, or before bed, regular use will help reinforce positive emotions and manage stress more effectively.

Questions for Reflection

- How often do you consciously manage your emotions throughout the day? What tools or strategies have been most effective for you?
- When you encounter a challenging situation, how do your attitude and emotional responses typically influence the outcome?
- What are some recurring negative emotional patterns you've noticed in your life, and how can you start shifting them to a more positive and empowering mindset?
- How can adopting a more positive attitude impact your relationships, career, and personal well-being in the long run?

Conclusion: Embrace the Power of Your Mind

Life is full of surprises, challenges, and opportunities. While you can't always control what happens, you can control how you respond to it. By cultivating a positive attitude and mastering emotional management, you unlock the potential to live a life that's not just happier, but more fulfilling.

Remember, these are skills that take practice. You won't wake up tomorrow with perfect emotional control or an unshakeable positive outlook—but every small step you take brings you closer to that goal. Start today, and over time, you'll find that you're living a life that's full of joy, peace, and possibility.

Now, go out there and make good things happen!

Final Reflection

Emotions may come and go, but your ability to influence and guide them shapes the quality of your life.

14
The Power of Belief and Consistent Action

Yes, I know, the road to success isn't always straightforward. Sometimes, we face setbacks, doubts, and obstacles that seem too big to overcome. In those moments, two things matter most: belief in yourself and consistent action. These are the cornerstones of success, and they work together like a powerhouse duo.

Let's explore why believing in yourself is more than just a motivational cliché, and how taking action—no matter how small—every day is the key to turning your dreams into reality.

The Power of Self-Belief: It All Starts with You

Belief is a force. It's the spark that ignites everything else in your life. When you believe in yourself, you unlock the mental and emotional strength to push through challenges, try new things, and step outside your comfort zone. Think about it: If you don't believe you can succeed, why would you even try?

The truth is, self-belief is the foundation for everything. It's the first step before any action or decision. It doesn't matter if you have all the tools, resources, or skills to succeed—if you don't believe you can, it's like having a car without fuel. You'll go nowhere.

The Science Behind Belief

Let's take a quick detour into psychology. There's a concept called the self-fulfilling prophecy. It means that when you strongly believe something—whether positive or negative—it tends to come true because your actions align with your belief. For example, if you believe you're destined to fail, you're more likely to avoid taking risks, give up too soon, or not put in your best effort. On the flip side, if you believe you're capable of succeeding, you'll act with confidence, push harder, and persevere through setbacks.

Your beliefs shape your reality. This doesn't mean you can sit on the couch, close your eyes, and magically manifest success. But it does mean that the way you see yourself directly influences how you behave and, ultimately, the results you get.

Why You Might Not Believe in Yourself (Yet)

Let's be real: Believing in yourself is easier said than done, right? A lot of us struggle with self-doubt, and that's completely normal. Maybe you've failed before and now you're scared of trying again. Or maybe you've grown up hearing things like "You're not smart enough" or "That's impossible for someone like you," and those limiting beliefs have stuck around.

Here's the good news: Self-belief is a skill. It's something you can build, strengthen, and grow over time. You don't need to be born with it. It's not pretending to be confident when you're not but developing a mindset that supports your success instead of undermining it.

Consistent Action: The Secret to Achieving Anything

Alright, so belief is the foundation. But belief alone won't get you across the finish line. You need to pair it with something crucial: consistent action. You might have heard the saying, "Success is the sum of small efforts, repeated day in and day out." This is where the magic happens.

Consistency is the quiet, often underestimated force that creates lasting change. It's not about doing something massive once and expecting results. It's about doing the small things, the unglamorous things, the hard things—again and again—until they add up to something big.

Why Consistency Beats Talent

Let's get this straight: Talent is great, but it's not the deciding factor for success. Plenty of talented people never reach their potential because they don't consistently put in the work. Meanwhile, people who are less naturally gifted can achieve incredible things simply by showing up day after day.

Consistency builds momentum. Think of it like pushing a boulder up a hill. The first few steps are hard, slow, and maybe even discouraging. But as you keep pushing, it gets a little easier, and eventually, you reach the point where that boulder starts rolling on its own. That's the power of consistency—small actions snowball into big results.

Start Small and Build Momentum

Here's something we've talked about throughout the book and where a lot of people get stuck: they think they need to make huge, dramatic changes all at once. But that's overwhelming, and it rarely sticks. Instead, start small. Focus on taking just one tiny step every day. It could be as simple as spending 10 minutes on a project, sending one email, or making one phone call. Over time, these small actions add up and create massive progress.

That is the power of consistency—small actions snowball into big results.

How Belief and Action Work Together

Now that we've covered belief and action separately, let's talk about how they work together.

When you believe in yourself, you take action with confidence. And when you take consistent action, it reinforces your belief in yourself. It's a powerful feedback loop. The more action you take, the more you prove to yourself that you're capable, and the stronger your belief becomes. And as your belief strengthens, you're more likely to take even bolder actions.

For example, imagine you're trying to start a business. At first, you might doubt yourself—"What if this fails?" But if you push past that fear and take action (even small steps like setting up a website or making your first sale), you'll start to see progress. That progress boosts your confidence, and now you're motivated to take even bigger actions.

Practical Tips to Strengthen Your Belief and Stay Consistent

It's all well and good to talk about belief and action, but how do you actually put this into practice? Let's break it down into some actionable steps.

Strengthening Your Belief in Yourself

- **Affirmations That Work**: Start your day with positive affirmations. Instead of generic phrases like, "I am successful," try something specific to your goals: "I have the creativity and skills to grow my business." These statements will help rewire your brain over time.

- **Visualize Your Success**: Spend a few minutes each day imagining what success looks and feels like. Picture yourself reaching your goal—what does that look like? How do you feel? Visualization helps solidify your belief that success is possible for you.

- **Surround Yourself with Positive Influences**: Who you spend time with matters. Surround yourself with people who believe in you and who encourage your growth. Avoid those who are constantly negative or doubtful. Their energy can hold you back.

Taking Consistent Action

- **Set Small, Achievable Goals**: Break down your big goals into smaller, more manageable tasks. For example, if you want to write a book, start by committing to writing 300 words a day. Small goals are less intimidating and easier to stick to.

- **Create a Routine**: Consistency thrives on routine. Set aside time every day (or every week) to work on your goals. Whether it's 30 minutes in the morning or an hour before bed, creating a habit around your actions makes it easier to stay consistent.

- **Track Your Progress**: Keep a journal or use an app to track your daily actions. Seeing how far you've come, even if the steps seem small, gives you motivation to keep going.

Real-Life Example: Putting It All Together

Let's look at a real-life scenario. Say you want to get in shape and improve your fitness. You believe you can do it, but the results seem far away. How do belief and consistent action work together in this case?

- **Step 1: Build Belief**: Remind yourself why you're capable of getting fit. Maybe you've succeeded in other areas of your life or improved your health in small ways before. Visualize yourself stronger, healthier, and more energetic. Affirm: "I am capable of becoming the healthiest version of myself."

- **Step 2: Take Consistent Action**: Start with manageable steps. Commit to exercising for just 10 minutes a day. It could be walking, stretching, or lifting weights. It doesn't have to be perfect—just consistent.

- **Step 3: Reinforce Belief Through Action**: As you stick to your routine, you'll start to see and feel the benefits—maybe your energy improves or your clothes fit better. This progress reinforces your belief that you can get in shape, making you even more motivated to keep going.

Before you know it, you'll have built both the mindset and the habits that lead to lasting success.

Exercises to Apply These Principles in Your Life

Daily Affirmations

Each morning, write down three positive affirmations that support your belief in yourself. For example:

- "I am capable of achieving my goals."
- "I have the skills and dedication to succeed."
- "I am becoming more confident every day."

Read them aloud to yourself before you start your day.

Action Journal

At the end of each day, write down one action you took towards your goal, no matter how small. This helps build the habit of consistent action and keeps you focused on progress.

Visualization Practice

Set aside five minutes each day to visualize yourself achieving your goal. Close your eyes and imagine every detail—what you see, how you feel, and the actions you took to get there. This strengthens your belief and keeps you motivated.

▶ Immediate Action: The Two-Minute Rule for Overcoming Procrastination

Procrastination can be one of the biggest obstacles to achieving your goals. Often, the thought of starting a task can feel overwhelming, leading to feelings of self-doubt and inaction. This exercise is designed to help you break that cycle and take the first steps toward your goals using the Two-Minute Rule—a powerful strategy that can transform your mindset and your productivity.

Step 1: Identify Your Procrastination Triggers: Begin by reflecting on tasks you've been putting off. Are there specific projects, goals, or responsibilities that consistently get delayed? Write down at least three of these tasks. Understanding what triggers your procrastination is essential. It may be due to fear of failure, perfectionism, or simply feeling overwhelmed. Recognizing these triggers is the first step toward conquering them.

Step 2: Choose a Task and Set a Timer: From your list, pick one task that you find particularly daunting. This could be anything from starting a workout routine, writing a report, or organizing your workspace. Once you've chosen the task, set a timer for two minutes. The idea here is to make the task feel manageable and less intimidating. Remember, you are only committing to two minutes of focused action—an achievable goal!

Step 3: Engage Fully in the Task: When the timer starts, engage fully in the task for those two minutes. If you chose to start exercising, put on your workout clothes and do a few stretches or light movements. If it's writing, open your document and jot down any thoughts or ideas related to the topic. Focus entirely on that small action—don't worry about completing the task, just immerse yourself in those two minutes.

Step 4: Reflect on Your Experience: After the timer goes off, take a moment to reflect on your experience. How did you feel during those two minutes? Were you surprised at how easy it was to start? Write down your thoughts in a journal. This reflection helps reinforce the positive feelings associated with taking action, making it easier to overcome procrastination in the future.

Step 5: Continue If You Feel Motivated: Often, the hardest part is just starting. Once you begin, you may find that you want to keep going beyond the two minutes. If that happens, allow yourself to continue working on the task. You'll likely find that after just two minutes, your momentum will carry you forward, and you'll be able to accomplish much more than you initially intended.

Step 6: Make it a Daily Habit: To maximize the effectiveness of the Two-Minute Rule, try to implement it daily. Choose a different task each day that you've been putting off. The more you practice this, the easier it will become to start tasks, and the more consistent your actions will be.

Over time, you'll develop a habit of tackling your responsibilities rather than avoiding them. You'll also reinforce your self-belief and build confidence in your ability to take action, regardless of how daunting a task may seem.

Questions for Reflection

- Self-Belief Assessment: What are some specific beliefs you hold about your abilities? Are these beliefs empowering or limiting? How can you shift them toward a more positive perspective?
- Identifying Consistent Actions: Reflect on your daily routine. What small actions are you currently taking that contribute to your goals? Are there additional small steps you could incorporate to enhance your progress?
- Overcoming Obstacles: What obstacles have you faced that have hindered your belief in yourself? How can you reframe these challenges to view them as opportunities for growth instead of setbacks?
- Support Systems: Who in your life encourages your self-belief and consistent action? How can you strengthen these relationships or seek out more positive influences?
- Visualization Practice: Spend a moment visualizing your success. What does achieving your goals feel like? How can this visualization help reinforce your belief in yourself?

Conclusion: Believe and Act Your Way to Success

Success is not a distant dream reserved for the lucky few. It's the result of two powerful forces that are available to all of us: belief in yourself and consistent action. When you combine these, you create an unstoppable momentum that drives you towards your goals, no matter how big they are.

You don't have to be the most talented or having all the resources, you need to truly believe you can achieve your dreams and then take action, day after day, to make them a reality. Start today—no matter how small—and you'll be amazed at what you can accomplish.

Final Reflection

Every great achievement begins with a single step taken in belief.

15

Resilience and Faith — The Unbreakable Combination to Overcome Adversity

Life can hit hard sometimes. We all go through moments of pain, confusion, and hardship. Maybe you've faced loss, betrayal, or failure. Or perhaps, like many people, you've struggled with the unexpected curveballs that life throws at you—financial struggles, personal challenges, or health issues. When you're in the thick of it, it's easy to feel like you're breaking down, like the world is too much to handle. But here's the truth: You are far more resilient than you think.

Resilience is your ability to bounce back, to get up after life has knocked you down. This isn't a question of being tough all the time or pretending you're unaffected. It's a question of having the strength to rebuild, to continue moving forward even when things feel impossible. And faith—whether that's faith in yourself, in a higher power, or in the goodness of life—is what fuels that resilience. Together, resilience and faith form the core of what it means to be unbreakable.

In this chapter, we're going to break down how these two powerful forces can help you rise above adversity, how you can develop them within yourself, and how to apply these principles to your everyday life so that no matter what comes your way, you're ready to face it with courage and hope.

What Is Resilience, Really?

Being resilient doesn't mean being invincible, never feeling pain or never getting knocked down. On the contrary, resilience is the ability to experience life's challenges and setbacks fully, but then decide not to let them define or destroy you. It's your capacity to adapt, to learn from what went wrong, and to grow stronger because of it.

Think of resilience like a muscle. You don't just wake up one day with unshakable resilience—it's something you build over time, through experience and intentional effort. Each time you face a difficulty and choose to keep going, you're training that resilience muscle. The more you flex it, the stronger it gets.

The Key Components of Resilience:

- **Emotional Strength**: You allow yourself to feel your emotions—whether it's sadness, frustration, or anger—without letting them consume you. Resilient people know that emotions are part of the process, but they don't let them dictate every action.

- **Problem-Solving**: Instead of seeing adversity as a dead end, resilient individuals look for solutions. They're focused on figuring out how to navigate around obstacles instead of being paralyzed by them.

- **Optimism**: This isn't blind positivity or pretending everything's fine when it's not but believing that things will eventually get better, and that setbacks are temporary, not permanent.

Resilience is your capacity to adapt, to learn from what went wrong, and to grow stronger because of it.

Faith: The Fuel for Resilience

Faith is the inner belief that no matter how dark things get, there is always a path forward. It's not just religious faith—although for some, that's a huge part of it. Faith can mean faith in yourself, in the people you love, in the universe, or simply in the idea that things will improve.

Faith is what keeps you going when you can't see the end of the tunnel. It's what stops you from giving up when everything in you is screaming to quit. Having faith is like having a compass that keeps pointing you in the right direction, even when the storm clouds roll in.

How Faith Supports Resilience:

- **Gives Meaning to Suffering**: When you have faith, you see challenges as something that can be overcome and as part of your greater story. Faith helps you believe that even in your pain, there is growth and purpose.

- **Increases Emotional Endurance**: With faith, you're better equipped to handle prolonged difficulties. Faith says, "It won't always be this hard. This too shall pass."

- **Offers a Sense of Community**: Faith often connects you to others, whether it's through shared belief systems or through people who support your journey. Knowing you're not alone can make all the difference.

Resilience in Action: Real-Life Examples

Let's consider some real-life scenarios where resilience and faith shine through.

Example 1: The Entrepreneur Who Failed (Multiple Times)

Imagine Sarah, an entrepreneur with big dreams of starting her own business. She launches her first startup, but it quickly falls apart due to poor planning. Determined to succeed, she tries again. The second business fails due to lack of funding. At this point, many people would give up, but Sarah doesn't. Instead, she takes each failure as a learning opportunity. She adjusts her strategy, seeks advice from others, and finally, on her third attempt, she builds a thriving company.

Sarah's resilience didn't mean she avoided failure. It meant she kept getting up and trying again. Her faith in herself and in the process fueled her determination, even when others told her it was time to give up.

Example 2: The Athlete Who Faced Injury

Now, take Rafael, a professional tennis player who suffered a career-threatening injury. For months, he was told he might never play again. The physical pain was one thing, but the emotional toll was devastating. Still, Rafael believed in his ability to heal. He leaned on his faith, trusting that this setback was part of his journey, not the end. Day by day, he worked hard in physical therapy, stayed mentally strong, and eventually returned to the game—stronger than before.

Rafael's resilience came from his refusal to accept defeat. His faith gave him hope and motivation to push through the tough times.

How to Build Your Own Resilience

Here's the thing: adversity is inevitable. Whether we like it or not, life will throw challenges our way. But we have a choice in how we respond. So how do you develop resilience in your own life? Let's break it down:

Change Your Perspective

One of the most powerful ways to build resilience is by shifting your mindset. Instead of seeing adversity as something to avoid, start viewing it as a chance to grow. Ask yourself, "What can I learn from this experience?" and "How can I become stronger because of this?" When you see challenges as opportunities for growth, they lose some of their power over you.

Take Small Steps Every Day

Resilience doesn't mean making one grand gesture in the face of adversity. Resilience is taking small, consistent steps forward. Whether it's getting out of bed on a tough day, reaching out to a friend for support, or simply reminding yourself that you're doing the best you can—every small step counts. Over time, these small acts build a powerful momentum.

Practice Self-Compassion

Being resilient doesn't consist of being hard on yourself. In fact, one of the most important aspects of resilience is self-compassion. Understand that it's okay to struggle. It's okay to feel overwhelmed. Give yourself permission to feel what you're feeling without judgment. Treat yourself with the same kindness you would offer to a close friend in a difficult time.

Strengthening Your Faith in Times of Struggle

Building faith can be challenging, especially when things aren't going your way. But faith, like resilience, is something you can strengthen over time. Here's how:

Focus on What You Can Control. In moments of hardship, it's easy to feel powerless. But one way to cultivate faith is by focusing on what you can control. You might not be able to change your circumstances overnight, but you can control your response. You can choose to keep moving forward, no matter how small the steps.

Find Meaning in Adversity. One way to build faith is by finding meaning in your struggles. Ask yourself: "How is this experience shaping the way I approach future challenges?" or "In what ways is this challenge revealing strengths I didn't know I had?" Faith is often about believing that even in your darkest moments, there is a purpose to your pain.

Lean on Your Support System. Faith is often reinforced by community. Whether you lean on family, friends, or a faith-based group, having people who believe in you can make all the difference. When your faith falters, let others lift you up.

Practical Exercises to Build Resilience and Strengthen Faith

Journaling for Resilience

Start a resilience journal. Every evening, write down one challenge you faced that day and how you responded to it. Reflect on what you learned from the experience and how it has made you stronger. This practice will help you reframe adversity as growth and build your resilience muscle.

Visualization for Faith

Each morning, spend five minutes visualizing yourself overcoming the challenges you're currently facing. Picture yourself stronger, more confident, and capable. Imagine how good it will feel when you've made it through. Visualization is a powerful tool to strengthen your faith in yourself and your journey.

Gratitude Practice

At the end of each day, write down three things you're grateful for, even if they're small. Gratitude helps shift your focus from what's going wrong to what's going right, building both resilience and faith.

▸ Immediate Action: Cultivate Resilience Through Reflection and Action

Resilience and faith are like the roots and wings that keep you grounded yet uplifted during life's challenges. This exercise will help you recognize your inner strength and deepen your faith so you can navigate adversity with confidence.

Identify a Recent Challenge: Think about a recent situation in which you felt overwhelmed or knocked down by life. Write down the details of the challenge, how you initially responded, and what emotions it triggered. This reflection is crucial in building self-awareness.

Shift the Narrative: Take a moment to recognize how this challenge is shaping you. Write down how you have grown, or could grow, because of this situation. Ask yourself: "What lesson is this teaching me? How is this helping me become stronger?" Even if you're still in the thick of the struggle, shifting the narrative from 'Why is this happening to me?' to 'What can I learn from this?' is a powerful act of resilience.

Take a Small Step Forward: Resilience is about forward motion, no matter how small. What is one small, manageable step you can take today to address this challenge? It could be something simple, like reaching out for help, setting a boundary, or even committing to a moment of self-care. Take that step today and reflect on how it felt afterward.

Strengthen Your Faith with a Mantra: Create a personal mantra that reflects your faith in yourself or in the process of overcoming adversity. Examples might include: "I trust in my ability to rise above this," or "This too shall pass, and I will grow through it." Repeat this mantra throughout the day whenever you feel doubt creeping in. This affirmation helps reinforce your faith and keeps you grounded in the knowledge that things will improve over time.

Track Your Resilience: Every day for the next week, journal one instance where you noticed your resilience—whether it's staying calm in the face of stress, bouncing back from disappointment, or even just getting through a hard day. By documenting these moments, you build evidence of your inner strength, reinforcing your belief in yourself.

This exercise encourages you to actively build resilience while reinforcing your faith in the process of growth and healing.

Questions for Reflection

- How have past challenges shaped the person you are today? Reflect on a difficult time in your life. What strengths or insights did you gain from that experience? How did it help you grow?

- In moments of adversity, how do you usually respond? Do you tend to retreat, push through, or seek support? How can you improve your response to challenges moving forward?

- What does faith mean to you in the context of resilience? Is your faith grounded in yourself, a higher power, or the belief that things will get better? How does this faith fuel your ability to keep going?

- When faced with a difficult situation, what small action can you take to move forward? Think of a current challenge. What is one simple step you can take today to begin overcoming it?

- How can you build resilience in your daily life? Consider small ways to exercise resilience, such as embracing discomfort, learning from mistakes, or practicing patience. How can you incorporate these practices into your routine?

Conclusion: Unbreakable You

Resilience and faith are not just traits you're born with—they're qualities you can build, strengthen, and cultivate. Life will throw challenges your way, but with resilience, you have the strength to bounce back. And with faith, you have the belief that no matter how tough things get, there's always hope for a better tomorrow.

Resilience is a matter of getting back up every time you do. And faith? It's what gives you the strength to rise. Embrace these two forces, and you'll find that nothing can break you.

Now, take these principles and start applying them to your life. Challenge yourself to grow, to believe, and to keep moving forward—even when the road gets tough.

You are capable of more than you realize.

Final Reflection

When life feels overwhelming, consider this: What if every challenge you face is an opportunity to discover the depth of your own power?

16
Why Financial Education Matters

Let's face it: money is something we all deal with, whether we like it or not. We need it to pay for the basics like food, shelter, and clothing. But beyond the essentials, money also gives us freedom. It allows us to live the life we want, pursue our dreams, and support the people we care about. Yet, here's the irony: despite its importance, most of us are never really taught how to manage it. We go through years of schooling, learning everything from algebra to history, but there's rarely a class on how to handle our personal finances. And that's a problem.

Financial independence doesn't just happen by accident. It's something you have to learn, plan for, and actively work toward. And the foundation of that journey is financial education—understanding how money works and how to make it work for you. This chapter will break down why financial education is so crucial and how it can change your entire relationship with money, setting you up for a life of financial independence, rather than a lifetime of paycheck-to-paycheck living.

The Difference Between Working for Money and Making Money Work for You

One of the first things to understand about money is that there are two main ways people approach it: working for money and making money work for you. Most people, whether they realize it or not, are stuck in the first category—they work for money. They go to a job, put in their hours, and get paid. There's nothing wrong with that, but here's the catch: if you only ever work for money, then you're dependent on your job to survive. If something happens—like losing that job or getting sick—your income stops, and suddenly, you're in trouble.

Now, compare that with making money work for you. This is where financial education comes into play. It's the idea that you can use money as a tool to generate more money, through investments, businesses, or assets that grow in value. When you understand how to make money work for you, you're no longer completely dependent on your job. You can have multiple streams of income, and those streams continue even when you're not actively working. It's the path to financial independence.

The Importance of Assets vs. Liabilities

If you want to achieve financial independence, one of the most important concepts to grasp is the difference between assets and liabilities. Once you understand this distinction, you can start making smarter decisions about how you spend and invest your money.

Assets: These are things that put money in your pocket. They generate income or increase in value over time. Examples include stocks, real estate, businesses, and intellectual property. Assets help you build wealth because they work for you, even when you're not working.

Liabilities: These are things that take money out of your pocket. They cost you money to own or maintain. A mortgage, a car loan, and credit card debt are all examples of liabilities. While some liabilities may seem like necessities (like a home or a car), they still drain your finances if they don't generate income.

Many people confuse liabilities with assets. For example, they might think their house is an asset, but if it's costing them money every month and not generating any income, it's actually a liability.

Shift Your Mindset: Stop Thinking Like an Employee, Start Thinking Like an Investor

One of the biggest mental shifts you need to make to achieve financial independence is to stop thinking solely like an employee. Employees work for others and are typically focused on earning a steady paycheck. Investors, on the other hand, look for ways to make their money grow. They focus on opportunities that will bring long-term financial rewards, even if they require more risk or initial effort.

Let's take an example: imagine you get a $5,000 bonus at work. The typical employee mindset might be to celebrate by spending it on a vacation, new clothes, or even paying off some debt. But an investor's mindset would see that $5,000 as an opportunity. Instead of spending it, they might invest it in stocks, start a small side business, or even put it toward a down payment on a rental property that could generate passive income.

It's not that you shouldn't enjoy your money or reward yourself for hard work, but if you're serious about financial independence, the majority of your decisions should be focused on growing your wealth, not just spending it.

Why Saving Alone Isn't Enough

You've probably been told at some point in your life that saving money is the key to financial success. And while saving is important, it's not enough on its own to achieve financial independence. Here's why: saving money in a traditional savings account barely grows. With low-interest rates and inflation eating away at your purchasing power, simply saving doesn't allow your money to grow over time.

Investing is what makes the difference. When you invest, you're giving your money the potential to grow through the power of compound interest, appreciation, and reinvestment. It's like planting seeds—each investment has the potential to grow into something much larger over time.

The Power of Passive Income

Passive income is the holy grail of financial independence. It's income that you earn without actively working for it. Once it's set up, it continues to flow, giving you financial security and freedom. There are many ways to create passive income, including:

Real Estate: Owning rental properties can generate monthly cash flow without requiring you to be involved in the day-to-day operations.

Investments: Stocks, bonds, and mutual funds can provide dividends and capital gains that grow over time.

Digital Products: If you create something like an online course or an e-book, you can sell it repeatedly without creating new material each time.

Businesses: Starting a business that can run independently, or investing in other businesses, can also provide passive income.

> *Passive income is the holy grail of financial independence.*

The beauty of passive income is that it frees up your time. Once your money is working for you, you're no longer trading hours for dollars, which is the key to financial freedom.

Common Financial Mistakes to Avoid

On the path to financial independence, there are some common mistakes that can trip you up. Here's what to watch out for:

Living beyond your means: If you're always spending more than you earn, you'll never get ahead financially. Cut unnecessary expenses and live within your means so you can use extra money to invest.

Getting into debt: High-interest debt, like credit card debt, is a financial killer. Pay off debt as quickly as possible and avoid taking on new debt unless it's for an investment that will generate income.

Relying on one source of income: Depending solely on your job for income is risky. Diversify your income streams through side hustles, investments, and passive income opportunities.

Not investing early enough: The earlier you start investing, the more time your money has to grow. Don't wait for the "perfect time" to start—time in the market is more important than timing the market.

Practical Exercises to Get Started on Your Path to Financial Independence

Now that we've covered some of the basics, it's time to take action. Below are some practical steps to help you start your journey toward financial independence.

Track Your Spending

Start by understanding where your money is going. For one month, track every expense—big or small. This will help you identify areas where you're overspending and opportunities to save or invest more.

Calculate Your Net Worth

To get a clear picture of your financial health, calculate your net worth. List all your assets (cash, savings, investments, property) and all your liabilities (debt, loans, credit card balances). Subtract your liabilities from your assets to get your net worth. This is your starting point, and from here, you can set goals to increase your net worth over time.

Create a Budget with an Investment Focus

Once you have a clear idea of your spending, create a budget that prioritizes saving and investing. Aim to allocate at least 20-30% of your income toward investments or debt repayment. Remember, the goal is to make your money work for you.

Start Building an Emergency Fund

Before diving into investments, it's important to have a safety net. Build an emergency fund with 3-6 months' worth of living expenses in case of job loss, medical emergencies, or unexpected expenses. This will give you peace of mind and prevent you from going into debt.

Educate Yourself on Investments

Start learning about different types of investments—stocks, bonds, real estate, and mutual funds. Choose one area that interests you and dive deeper. There are countless resources available online, from podcasts to YouTube channels, that can teach you the basics of investing.

▶ Immediate Action: Create Your Personal Investment Strategy

Develop a basic personal investment strategy:

Set Your Financial Goals

Take 15-30 minutes to write down clear, measurable financial goals. Ask yourself:

- How much money do you want to accumulate in the next 5, 10, and 20 years?

- What are your priorities (e.g., retirement, purchasing a home, building passive income)?

- What kind of lifestyle do you want your investments to support?

Define Your Risk Tolerance

Next, understand your risk tolerance. Ask yourself:

- Are you comfortable with the possibility of short-term losses for long-term gains?

- How much fluctuation in your investment value can you handle without panicking? If you're risk-averse, you might lean toward conservative investments like bonds or index funds. If you're open to more risk, explore stocks, real estate, or even startups.

Research Investment Types

Pick one type of investment to start with (e.g., stocks, mutual funds, real estate). Spend at least one hour researching:

- How it works

- What kind of returns you can expect over time

- How much money you need to begin Use free resources such as reputable websites, podcasts, or books to build your understanding.

Start Small with Your First Investment

With your research done, take the first step and make a small investment. Whether it's buying a few shares of a stock, investing in a low-cost index fund, or purchasing a fraction of a rental property, commit to starting small. Use platforms with minimal fees, such as online brokers or investment apps.

Track Your Progress and Adjust

Set a recurring reminder to review your investments monthly. Track how they perform, and revisit your goals every six months. Adjust your investment strategy as your understanding grows and your financial situation changes.

Questions for Reflection

- What beliefs about money did you grow up with, and how have they influenced your financial decisions so far?

- Are you more focused on working for money or finding ways to make money work for you? How might this shift impact your financial future?

- When you consider your current spending habits, are you prioritizing investments in assets or liabilities? What small changes can you make to increase your focus on building assets?

- What is your relationship with risk? Are there areas where fear of failure is holding you back from making smarter financial decisions?

- How would achieving financial independence change your day-to-day life and your ability to pursue your passions or dreams?

Conclusion: Financial Education is Your Roadmap to Freedom

Financial independence isn't reserved for the lucky or the wealthy—it's something anyone can achieve with the right mindset and education. By understanding how money works, differentiating between assets and liabilities, and learning how to make your money work for you, you can create a life of freedom and security.

You don't have to figure it all out today. The important thing is to start. Each step you take toward educating yourself and making smarter financial decisions will bring you closer to the life of independence you desire.

Are you ready to take control of your financial future? The power is in your hands.

Final Reflection

Financial independence is reclaiming your freedom. By educating yourself and taking control of your financial choices, you unlock the potential to live on your own terms, free from dependency or fear.

17

Balancing Material Success and Spiritual Fulfillment

We live in a world where the chase for success often feels like the main game. The more we hustle, the more we feel validated. Success becomes this shiny, towering goal that we imagine will bring us happiness, fulfillment, and peace. And while achieving material success does offer a sense of accomplishment, what happens when you get there? Why do so many people who "make it" still feel empty inside? The truth is, without a deeper sense of purpose or inner peace, success can feel hollow.

Finding the balance between material success and spiritual fulfillment is not about choosing one over the other. You don't have to give up all your worldly desires to feel spiritually connected, nor do you need to sacrifice your inner peace to be successful in life. The key is learning how to integrate both. This chapter explores how you can enjoy success in the material world while also nourishing your spirit, finding peace, joy, and purpose along the way.

What is Success, Really?

Let's start by redefining success. In today's world, success is often measured by external markers: how much money you have, the kind of house you live in, the car you drive, or how impressive your job title sounds. But true success goes far beyond these material symbols. It's about the feeling of contentment and joy that comes from within.

Success can also mean:

Waking up excited to start your day because you're doing work you love.

Feeling a deep sense of purpose in the relationships you build.

Maintaining a state of inner peace, even when life throws challenges your way.

Living in a way that aligns with your values, where your actions reflect the kind of person you want to be.

> *Without a deeper sense of purpose or inner peace, success can feel hollow.*

Material wealth is one kind of success, but spiritual fulfillment—feeling at peace, aligned with your purpose, and connected to something bigger than yourself—is a deeper, more lasting kind of success. True happiness comes when these two worlds are in balance.

The Importance of Inner Peace in a Fast-Paced World

The modern world moves fast. We're constantly bombarded with deadlines, emails, social media notifications, and a never-ending to-do list. It's easy to get caught up in this whirlwind of activity, but if you're not careful, the constant hustle can leave you feeling burned out and disconnected from yourself.

This is where inner peace becomes crucial. Inner peace is the ability to return to a calm, centered state even when things around you are chaotic. It's the space you create for yourself to breathe, reflect, and reconnect with what truly matters.

When you prioritize inner peace, you gain clarity. You stop making decisions based on fear or urgency and instead make choices aligned with your values. You begin to feel more grounded, more present, and more in tune with the flow of life.

How to Integrate Success and Spiritual Fulfillment

So, how do you strike that balance between external success and internal peace? The good news is, you don't have to choose between the two. You can be successful and spiritually fulfilled if you approach both with the right mindset and practices.

Redefine Your Idea of Wealth. Most people associate wealth purely with money, but true wealth encompasses so much more. Consider the following types of wealth:

- **Financial Wealth**: Having enough money to live comfortably and take care of yourself and your loved ones.

- **Time Wealth**: The freedom to spend your time as you choose, doing things you enjoy.

- **Emotional Wealth**: Being emotionally healthy and having fulfilling relationships.

- **Spiritual Wealth**: Feeling connected to your purpose, values, and a higher sense of meaning.

When you broaden your definition of wealth, you stop focusing solely on accumulating money and start seeking balance in all areas of life. Financial success is important, but it's just one piece of the puzzle.

Create Space for Stillness. In a busy world, stillness is a luxury. Take time each day to be still—whether through meditation, quiet reflection, or simply sitting in nature. This is when you can reconnect with your inner self and your purpose. These moments of stillness are where your most profound insights and creative ideas will emerge.

You don't have to set aside hours. Even just 5-10 minutes of quiet time can help you reset and return to your day with more clarity and calm.

Align Your Work with Your Purpose. One of the best ways to blend success with fulfillment is to ensure that your work aligns with your values and sense of purpose. Ask yourself:

- Does my work make a positive impact on others?

- Am I passionate about what I do, or am I simply doing it for the paycheck?

- Does my work allow me to grow, both personally and professionally?

When your work feels meaningful, it's no longer just a job—it becomes part of your spiritual journey. You'll find that success comes more naturally when you're doing work that lights you up inside.

Practice Gratitude for the Present Moment. Gratitude is a powerful practice that shifts your focus from what you lack to what you already have. It's easy to get caught up in the next goal, the next achievement, or the next material possession. But when you take time to appreciate what's already in your life, you create a deeper sense of fulfillment.

Detach from the Outcome. While it's important to set goals and work hard to achieve them, it's equally important to detach from the outcome. This doesn't mean you shouldn't care about the result, but rather that you shouldn't let your happiness depend on it.

When you're too attached to a specific outcome, you create unnecessary stress and pressure. But when you trust that things will unfold as they're meant to, you allow yourself to enjoy the process. The journey becomes as valuable as the destination.

Practical Exercises to Find Your Balance

Let's now dive into some practical exercises to help you apply these ideas in your life.

Clarify Your Definition of Success

Take a few minutes to reflect on what success means to you beyond material wealth. Write down your definition, including areas like relationships, personal growth, and inner peace. This will serve as your guidepost as you move forward.

Create a Daily Gratitude Practice

Start each day by writing down three things you're grateful for. As we talked, these can be simple things, like a good meal or a productive day at work. Over time, this practice will help you appreciate both the small and large blessings in your life.

Schedule Time for Stillness

Find 10 minutes each day to sit quietly without distractions. Use this time to reflect, meditate, or simply breathe. This small habit can have a profound impact on your ability to find peace and clarity.

Reassess Your Work-Life Alignment

Think about your current job or career. Does it bring you fulfillment beyond the paycheck? If not, explore ways you can bring more purpose into your work. Maybe it's finding more meaningful projects or even considering a career change.

▶ Immediate Action: Set a Goal and Practice Detachment from the Outcome

This practice encourages enjoyment in the process and reduces stress related to outcomes.

Identify Your Goal:

Choose one personal or professional goal that you genuinely want to achieve. It could be anything from completing a project at work, developing a new skill, or improving your health.

Write It Down:

Clearly articulate your goal in writing. Use the SMART criteria (Specific, Measurable, Achievable, Relevant, Time-bound) to ensure it's well-defined. For example: "I will exercise for 30 minutes three times a week for the next month."

Reflect on the Why:

Take a moment to reflect on why this goal is important to you. Write down your reasons for pursuing it, focusing on how it aligns with your values and contributes to your sense of fulfillment.

Set a Timeline:

Determine a reasonable timeframe to work toward your goal. Break it down into smaller milestones or checkpoints along the way. For instance, if your goal is to exercise regularly, plan weekly targets and track your progress.

Commit to the Process:

Focus on the actions you will take rather than the final result. Outline specific steps you will take each week to move toward your goal. Write these actions down as a commitment to yourself.

Practice Non-Attachment:

Remind yourself that while achieving the goal is important, the value lies in the experiences and lessons learned throughout the process. Acknowledge that external factors may influence the outcome, and that's okay.

Regular Check-Ins:

Set aside time each week to reflect on your progress. Instead of evaluating whether you have achieved your goal, assess how you feel about the actions you've taken and what you've learned along the way.

Celebrate the Journey:

At the end of your timeframe, regardless of the outcome, take time to celebrate the progress you made and the effort you put into the journey. Reflect on how you grew during this time, and recognize that growth and fulfillment are equally valuable.

Questions for Reflection

- What does success mean to you beyond material wealth? How can you redefine it in a way that resonates with your values?

- Reflect on a time when you achieved a goal but still felt unfulfilled. What aspects of your journey contributed to that feeling?

- How can you integrate moments of stillness into your daily routine? What practices might help you reconnect with your inner self?

- In what ways can you align your work with your sense of purpose? What steps can you take to infuse more meaning into your professional life?

- Consider your current goals—how attached are you to the outcomes? What would it feel like to focus more on the process instead?

Conclusion: Success is About Balance

At the end of the day, true success is about balance. You don't have to sacrifice one part of your life to gain fulfillment in another. When you take the time to nurture your inner world—your spirit, your peace, your sense of purpose—your outer world will reflect that richness. Material success is wonderful, but it's even more rewarding when it's combined with a deep sense of spiritual fulfillment.

Life is a journey. There will always be new goals, new challenges, and new opportunities. The key is to stay grounded in your purpose, stay present in the moment, and always strive for balance between what you do and who you are.

Final Reflection

Success is not merely defined by what you achieve but by how you feel while pursuing it.

18
Unlock Your Inner Power

Let's talk about something most of us don't realize: you are capable of way more than you give yourself credit for. Seriously. There's this incredible power inside of you that's been waiting to break out, but chances are you've been holding it back without even knowing it. Why? Because like most people, you've probably been stuck in the same old mental loops—thinking small, doubting yourself, and not truly believing that you deserve all the amazing things life has to offer.

But here's the deal: when you change your mindset and connect with the energy of the universe, you can unlock this inner greatness. I'm talking about realizing that the universe has your back, and everything you need to be awesome is already inside you. You just have to access it.

In this chapter, we'll break down exactly how to shift your mindset, connect with the universe, and start living the amazing life you were meant to live. No fluff, just practical steps to help you unleash the inner you that's ready to conquer the world.

The Power of Mindset: Why Everything Starts in Your Head

As you already know, your thoughts are shaping your reality. Think of your mind like a powerful magnet that's constantly pulling things into your life. The thoughts you think most often are the ones that have the most energy, and that energy attracts experiences that match up with them.

There's real power in this. When you shift your thoughts to focus on possibility, growth, and success, you open the door for those things to come into your life.

The universe has your back, and everything you need to be awesome is already inside you.

Your thoughts are like a blueprint, and your life is built based on that blueprint. If the blueprint is full of doubt and fear, your life will reflect that. But if the blueprint is filled with confidence, abundance, and self-belief, your reality will start to match up.

Connecting with the Universe: The Energy Behind Everything

Now let's talk about the universe. And no, this isn't about sitting in a room meditating until you float away (though meditation is awesome, I'll get to that again later). This is about recognizing that you are part of something way bigger than yourself.

The universe is full of energy—call it what you want: Source, God, the divine, cosmic consciousness—whatever resonates with you. The point is, this energy is available to you, and it's always there to support you. But to tap into this energy, you've got to be open to it.

Think of the universe as this massive Wi-Fi network. It's constantly sending out signals and guidance, but if you're not connected, you're missing out on all that wisdom. When you tune in, you start to notice synchronicities, opportunities, and ideas that come your way. You begin to realize that you're not alone in this. The universe has your back, but you need to plug into that flow.

Why the Universe Wants You to Succeed

Here's something you need to remember: the universe wants you to succeed. It's not testing you, and it's not holding anything back. In fact, it's constantly sending opportunities your way. The only thing standing between you and your dreams is your own resistance.

That resistance often shows up as fear—fear of failure, fear of rejection, fear of not being good enough. But here's the good news: fear is just a story. And like any story, it can be rewritten.

When you release your fears and align with the energy of the universe, you'll start to see doors open, people showing up at the right time, and ideas popping into your head. That's the universe saying, "Let's go! You've got this!"

Practical Exercises to Unlock Your Inner Power

Let's put this into practice. These exercises will help you shift your mindset, tap into universal energy, and start living like the powerful person you are.

Mindset Audit

For one day, carry a notebook with you and jot down any negative thoughts that pop into your mind. Be honest. At the end of the day, review them and write a positive affirmation to counter each one. For example, if you wrote down "They'll probably reject me, and I'll be embarrassed," your affirmation could be, "I am brave for expressing my true feelings, and I deserve love and connection regardless of the outcome."

Create a Morning Ritual

Start each day by spending 10 minutes in a positive headspace. This could include:

- A short meditation.

- Writing down 3 things you're grateful for.

- Saying your affirmations out loud.

- Visualizing your goals as if you've already achieved them.

This sets the tone for your day and aligns you with the energy of success and abundance.

Vision Board Creation

Spend an afternoon creating a vision board that represents the life you want to live. Cut out images, quotes, or symbols that resonate with your dreams—whether it's a new career, relationships, health goals, or anything else. Hang it somewhere you'll see it every day to remind yourself what you're working toward.

▶ Immediate Action: Follow the Breadcrumbs of Synchronicity

Begin your week by setting a clear intention to notice and recognize signs, opportunities, and synchronicities around you. You can write this intention in your journal or say it aloud: "I am open to receiving guidance and noticing the breadcrumbs the universe places in my path."

Prepare Your Tracking Tool

Choose a method to track your observations. This could be a dedicated notebook, a digital note on your phone, or a specific section in your journal. Ensure it's easily accessible so you can jot down thoughts quickly.

Stay Mindful Throughout the Day

As you go about your daily routine, practice mindfulness. Pay attention to your surroundings, conversations, and feelings. Stay open and curious about what you encounter. Ask yourself questions like, "What is this experience trying to teach me?" or "How is this relevant to my journey?"

Document Your Findings Daily

Each evening, take time to review your day and write down any signs, opportunities, or synchronicities you encountered. Examples could include:

- A chance encounter that sparked a new idea.
- An article or book you stumbled upon that resonated deeply.
- A phrase or piece of advice from a friend that made you think differently.

Reflect on Patterns

At the end of the week, read through your notes. Look for patterns or recurring themes. Ask yourself what these breadcrumbs might be guiding you toward. Consider questions like:

- Are there specific areas of your life where the universe is trying to direct your attention?
- Do any of the signs relate to goals or desires you have?

Take Inspired Action

Based on your reflections, identify one small action you can take that aligns with the signs and opportunities you noticed. This could be reaching out to someone you met, exploring a new interest, or making a decision that feels right based on your insights.

Share Your Experience

At the end of the week, consider sharing your experience with a friend or journaling about it. Discussing your discoveries can deepen your understanding and reinforce your connection to the universal energy guiding you.

By following these steps, you will become more attuned to the universe's messages and the hidden opportunities that can lead you closer to your goals and desires.

Questions for Reflection

- What beliefs or thought patterns have been holding you back from realizing your full potential?

- Can you identify moments of synchronicity in your life where events seemed to align perfectly? What did you learn from those experiences?

- How can you better connect with the energy of the universe in your daily life?

- In what ways can you shift your mindset to focus on possibility and abundance rather than fear and doubt?

- What specific steps can you take this week to notice and act upon the "breadcrumbs" of opportunity that come your way?

Conclusion: You're Already Unstoppable

The truth is, you don't need to become someone else to unlock your greatness. It's already inside you. You have everything you need to create an extraordinary life, but it starts with changing your mindset and plugging into the energy of the universe. When you shift your thoughts from fear to possibility, you align with a powerful flow that will guide you exactly where you need to go.

Final Reflection

Every moment is brimming with potential, waiting for you to tap into it. Your inner power is not a distant dream but a living force, ready to guide you toward the extraordinary life you deserve.

19

Mastering the Art of Caring Less: Focus on What Really Matters

Let's be honest: we care too much about things that don't matter. Whether it's what others think of us, keeping up with superficial goals, or obsessing over every tiny detail of life, we often waste energy on stuff that, in the grand scheme of things, just doesn't matter. It's time to cut through the noise and get real about where you're placing your energy.

The key to living a fulfilling life isn't doing more or being perfect. It's learning to care less about the things that don't serve you, and focusing your attention on what truly matters. Sounds simple, right? Yet, we complicate it. We let society's expectations, social media pressures, and outdated beliefs about success dictate how we feel, act, and think.

This chapter is about flipping that narrative on its head and getting rid of the mental clutter and zooming in on the things that truly make a difference. Let's dive into how you can stop worrying so much about the things that don't matter, and start focusing on what truly brings meaning to your life.

The Power of Not Caring: Freeing Yourself From the Unnecessary

Imagine for a moment that your mind is like a computer. Just like a computer has a limited amount of memory, so do you. If you try to run too many programs at once or overload it with too much data, it slows down, gets overwhelmed, and eventually crashes.

Your brain works the same way. When you're constantly caring about everything—your appearance, what your neighbor thinks, whether you have the latest gadget, or how many likes your Instagram post got—you're spreading your mental resources too thin. You're wasting your limited time and energy on things that don't actually make a difference in your life.

But what if you could be selective? What if you could choose to stop caring about all the superficial things that drain your energy, and instead focus on the things that bring you joy, fulfillment, and growth?

I'm not talking about being lazy or apathetic but reclaiming your attention and using it wisely. Think of it as a sort of "mental minimalism"—letting go of the emotional junk that clutters your mind so you can focus on the things that bring true meaning.

How to Know What to Care About

Before you can start caring less, you need to figure out what truly deserves your attention.

This sounds obvious, but it's trickier than it seems because, let's face it, we've been conditioned to care about a lot of things that don't really matter.

Here's how you figure out what's worth your energy:

Ask Yourself: Does This Matter in the Long Run? Think about the things that stress you out daily. Will they still matter in five years? Next year? Next month? If the answer is no, it's probably not worth worrying about. For example, the opinion of that random coworker you barely interact with? That doesn't matter in the long run. Your mental and physical health? That matters a lot.

Evaluate What Aligns with Your Values. What are the core values that drive you? Family, creativity, personal growth, honesty? When you align your focus with your values, you'll notice that a lot of distractions start to fall away. If something doesn't support your values, why waste time on it?

Decide What Brings You Joy or Fulfillment. It's easy to get stuck in a routine of doing things just because we think we should, but does that actually bring you joy or satisfaction? Start caring more about the things that make you feel alive and less about the obligations that drain you.

Prioritize Growth Over Comfort. Sometimes we care too much about staying comfortable—whether it's avoiding difficult conversations or not taking risks. But often, the things that push us out of our comfort zone lead to the most growth. Care more about the things that challenge and stretch you, and less about what feels "safe."

> *Start caring more about the things that make you feel alive and less about the obligations that drain you.*

The Art of Selective Caring: Choosing Your Battles Wisely

The truth is, you can't stop caring about everything—nor should you. It's about being selective. Life is full of things that demand your attention, but it's up to you to decide where to invest your limited energy.

Let's say you're constantly worrying about your job. You put in long hours, stress about every meeting, and feel like you're always one mistake away from disaster. But when you take a step back, you realize that your career isn't actually aligned with what makes you happy. It's not fulfilling, and no matter how hard you work, it doesn't give you a sense of purpose.

Instead of burning yourself out trying to please your boss or climb the corporate ladder, why not redirect your energy toward something that does matter to you? Maybe it's a side project, a hobby, or spending more time with your loved ones. You're still putting in effort, but now it's going toward something that feels meaningful.

Here's the key: Choosing your battles doesn't mean avoiding responsibility. It means focusing on the right responsibilities.

Life will always throw challenges at you. The trick is knowing which ones are worth your time. If you're constantly stressed about things like what people think of you, trying to control everything, or worrying about things outside of your control (hello, traffic), you're wasting precious energy.

When you focus on what you can control and let go of the rest, you free up mental space. You have more energy to focus on your relationships, your passions, and your personal growth.

Practical Exercises: How to Stop Worrying About the Wrong Things

Let's talk about how to actually put this into practice. Here are some exercises to help you start caring less about the unimportant stuff and more about the things that matter.

The Five-Year Test

When something stresses you out, ask yourself: "Will this matter in five years?" If the answer is no, it's a sign that you're over-investing your energy in something trivial. Next time you're obsessing over a minor inconvenience, like someone cutting you off in traffic or a mistake at work, take a breath and ask yourself this question.

List Your Values

Write down your top five core values. These could be anything from honesty and creativity to health and adventure. Then, compare this list with the things you spend most of your time worrying about. Do they align? If not, start making changes. For example, if family is one of your top values but you're spending 80% of your time stressing about work, it's time to rethink your priorities.

The "Yes or No" Rule

This is a great filter for deciding what's worth your energy. If an opportunity or activity doesn't make you say, "Oh yes!" then it's probably a "no." This can be anything from agreeing to social plans to taking on a new project at work. If it doesn't excite you or align with your values, why are you saying yes?

Weekly Reflection

At the end of each week, reflect on how you spent your time and energy. Ask yourself:

- What did I spend too much energy caring about?
- What should I have cared more about?
- Where can I make adjustments to focus on what truly matters?

This reflection practice will help you build awareness and gradually shift your focus to the things that bring real fulfillment.

Declutter Your Mental Space

Just like your physical space, your mind can get cluttered. Spend 10 minutes each day clearing out the mental clutter by writing down all your worries, to-dos, and random thoughts. Once it's on paper, ask yourself: "What's actually important here?" Often, you'll realize that a lot of your worries are unnecessary, and you can cross them off the list.

▶ Immediate Action: The "Energy Audit" Exercise

This exercise will help you become aware of where you're wasting energy on things that don't truly matter and redirect your focus toward what aligns with your values and goals.

Step 1: Create Two Lists

On a sheet of paper or in a journal, draw a line down the middle to create two columns. In the left column, write "Things I'm Currently Worrying About" and list everything that occupies your mind—whether it's work-related stress, relationships, social media, or even small daily inconveniences.

In the right column, write "Things That Truly Matter." Reflect on what genuinely aligns with your values and brings meaning to your life. Include things like personal growth, health, family, or fulfilling passions.

Step 2: Compare the Two Lists

Look at the first list and ask yourself: "Are these worries serving my long-term happiness and fulfillment?" Circle any items that don't align with the "Things That Truly Matter" column. These are the areas where you're investing too much mental energy unnecessarily.

Step 3: Make Conscious Shifts

Choose three items from the "worries" list that you're going to start caring less about. This could be something like the opinions of others, trivial work issues, or minor daily frustrations. Decide to consciously let go of these things by mentally committing to focusing less on them.

Step 4: Reinvest Your Energy

Now, identify three things from the "Things That Truly Matter" list where you want to reinvest the energy you've freed up. These should align with your core values, like spending more time with family, investing in your health, or working on a meaningful project.

Step 5: Daily Check-In

For the next seven days, spend five minutes each morning reviewing your two lists. Remind yourself of the things you're consciously choosing to care less about, and refocus your energy on the areas that truly matter.

This daily practice will help you gradually rewire your focus and live a life that aligns more with what genuinely fulfills you.

Questions for Reflection

- What are the things I often worry about that don't align with my core values?
- How does caring about insignificant matters affect my overall well-being and energy levels?

- In what areas of my life do I find myself seeking approval or validation from others, and how can I let go of that?

- Where can I start shifting my focus to invest more energy in the things that bring me true fulfillment?

- How can I embrace discomfort or challenges that lead to growth instead of wasting energy on staying comfortable?

Conclusion: The Freedom of Caring Less

Here's the truth: you don't have to care about everything. In fact, you shouldn't. The freedom to care less about the things that drain you, and more about the things that light you up, is one of the greatest gifts you can give yourself.

When you stop worrying about the opinions of others, about being perfect, or about every tiny detail that could go wrong, you open yourself up to a world of possibilities. You create space for growth, joy, and the things that actually make your life better.

So the next time you find yourself spiraling into a worry about something trivial, ask yourself: "Does this really matter?" And if the answer is no, let it go. Invest your energy where it counts, and you'll find yourself living a life with more freedom, more fulfillment, and way less stress.

Final Reflection

True freedom comes when you let go of what doesn't serve you. When you stop giving your energy to the unimportant, you make space for what truly matters.

20

The 80/20 Rule: Maximize Your Results with Less Effort

We've all heard the phrase "work smarter, not harder," but how do you actually do that? One of the most powerful ways is through something called the 80/20 rule. It's simple but incredibly impactful: 80% of your results come from just 20% of your efforts.

Think about that for a second. Most of the energy, time, and effort you're putting into your daily life or work isn't actually driving the results you want. If you can pinpoint and focus on that magical 20%, you can make a massive difference without burning yourself out.

But let's break it down. What does this really mean, and how can you apply it to your life?

Understanding the 80/20 Principle

The 80/20 principle—also called the Pareto Principle—is a universal law of imbalance. It suggests that in most areas of life, a small number of causes lead to the majority of outcomes. This applies to everything from business and relationships to learning and personal goals.

For example:

- In business, 20% of customers often generate 80% of the profits.

- In your personal relationships, 20% of your friendships bring you 80% of your joy.

- In learning a skill, 20% of the techniques you practice produce 80% of your improvement.

What's incredible about this principle is that it challenges the myth of equal input and output. Most of us assume that working longer hours or pushing harder will automatically lead to better results, but that's not the case. The 80/20 rule tells us that more effort doesn't always equal better results. The trick is to find that 20% of your actions that really move the needle.

> *A small number of causes lead to the majority of outcomes.*

How to Find Your 20%

The first step in using the 80/20 rule is to identify the most effective activities—the things that truly drive results. You need to sift through all the noise in your life and figure out which tasks are actually making an impact.

Let's walk through some practical steps to help you find your 20%.

1. Audit Your Time and Efforts

The best way to figure out where your results are coming from is to look at how you're spending your time and energy. Start by listing out all the activities you do in a day, a week, or a month. Whether it's work-related or personal, write down everything you spend time on.

Next, rate these activities based on their impact. Which ones are truly leading to tangible results, and which ones are more about maintaining the status quo or just staying busy?

For example, if you're running a small business, maybe you spend hours each day answering emails. But does that actually help you grow your business? Probably not. Now compare that to the time you spend talking to your top clients or brainstorming new product ideas. Those activities are likely making a much bigger impact.

2. Identify the Vital Few

Once you've audited your tasks, look for patterns. Ask yourself:

Which activities consistently give me the best results?

Where do I see the most progress or positive feedback?

For example, if you're a writer, you might notice that the time you spend outlining or drafting new ideas brings much more progress than the hours you spend perfecting tiny details in your writing. This insight can help you focus on producing more content, knowing that perfecting every little thing may not be worth the time.

3. Eliminate or Delegate the 80%

Here's the hard part—letting go of the things that aren't truly making an impact. This is where most people get stuck. We like to feel productive, and being busy often gives us a false sense of achievement. But if 80% of what you're doing isn't driving results, it's time to cut back.

Can you delegate these tasks to someone else? Can you automate them, or simply stop doing them altogether? For instance, if you're spending hours a week on administrative tasks that don't lead to growth, can you outsource those tasks to a virtual assistant?

4. Double Down on the 20%

Once you've identified the high-impact activities, the next step is to maximize your time and energy on those. This doesn't just mean doing more of them; it means optimizing how you do them.

For example, if you've figured out that 20% of your sales calls are closing 80% of your deals, look into what makes those calls different. Are you speaking to a different type of customer? Do you approach the conversation in a certain way? Double down on what's working and make it even more effective.

Practical Examples of the 80/20 Rule in Action

Fitness: Instead of spending hours at the gym, focus on the 20% of exercises that give you 80% of the results. Compound exercises like squats, deadlifts, and bench presses work multiple muscles at once, giving you more bang for your buck.

Relationships: Identify the 20% of people in your life who give you the most happiness and connection. Spend more time nurturing those relationships, and less time worrying about maintaining casual acquaintances that drain your energy.

Learning: If you're learning a new language, 20% of the vocabulary is used 80% of the time in everyday conversations. Focus on learning the most commonly used words and phrases first to accelerate your progress.

Business: In a workplace setting, you might find that 20% of your customers generate 80% of your revenue. Prioritize them by offering personalized service, while automating or streamlining interactions with lower-impact clients.

Exercises to Apply the 80/20 Rule

Let's get practical! Here are some exercises to help you apply the 80/20 rule to your own life.

Daily Task Audit

At the end of each day, list all the tasks you worked on. Rank them in terms of how much they contributed to your most important goals. Identify the top 20%—the tasks that had the biggest impact. Then, challenge yourself to focus on those top activities the next day.

Monthly Progress Review

At the end of the month, review your achievements. Look at the goals you hit and the progress you made. Write down the activities that contributed most to those successes. Were there things you spent time on that didn't move you forward? Make a plan to focus more on the impactful tasks in the next month.

The "Stop Doing" List

Create a "stop doing" list of tasks that fall into the 80%—those that aren't contributing significantly to your success or happiness. Whether it's checking your email every five minutes, micromanaging small details, or saying yes to every invitation, commit to cutting back on these time-sinks. Over time, you'll notice how much more energy you have for what really matters.

▶ Immediate Action: The 80/20 Quick Focus Reset

Identify and shift your focus toward the most impactful tasks in your day using the 80/20 principle.

Step 1: Identify Your Top 3 Goals for Today

At the start of your day, write down your three most important goals or tasks. These should be the things you need to accomplish that will make the biggest difference in your progress, whether it's for work, personal projects, or well-being.

Step 2: Audit Your Planned Tasks

Now, list out everything else you plan to do today. This could include meetings, errands, emails, or chores. Compare this list to your top 3 goals. Are any of these tasks likely to contribute significantly to those goals?

Step 3: Eliminate or Deprioritize

From the list of additional tasks, identify the ones that won't significantly contribute to your main goals or aren't urgent. Deprioritize them, eliminate them, or schedule them for later in the week. This will clear your schedule to focus on what matters most.

Step 4: Focus on Your High-Impact Tasks

Spend the majority of your time and energy today on tasks that support your top 3 goals. Whenever you find yourself tempted to switch to lower-priority activities, remind yourself that 80% of your results come from these key tasks.

Step 5: End-of-Day Review

At the end of the day, reflect on how it went. Did focusing on your high-impact tasks lead to better progress? Were there moments when you got distracted by less important tasks? Use this reflection to fine-tune your focus for the next day.

This daily reset helps you quickly prioritize and align your actions with what truly drives results, making the 80/20 principle an active part of your routine.

Questions for Reflection

- What tasks or activities in my life produce the most meaningful results? Have I identified the specific 20% that drives 80% of my progress in work, relationships, or personal growth?

- Am I spending time on things that give me little return? Which tasks or commitments consume my time and energy without significantly contributing to my goals or well-being?

- What patterns do I notice in my daily activities? Are there recurring tasks that consistently yield better results, and how can I prioritize them more effectively?

- How can I apply the 80/20 rule to my relationships? Which relationships bring me the most joy, fulfillment, and growth? How can I invest more time in these connections?

- What can I stop doing or delegate to free up time for high-impact tasks? Which responsibilities or habits can I let go of to focus more on the things that truly matter?

- How has my understanding of effort vs. results changed through applying the 80/20 principle? Do I feel more in control of my time and energy by focusing on fewer but more impactful actions?

Conclusion

The power of the 80/20 rule lies in its simplicity and effectiveness. By identifying the vital few actions that drive most of your results, you can cut through the noise and focus your energy where it truly counts. Life isn't about doing more, but about doing what matters most. When you embrace this mindset, you unlock the potential to achieve more with less effort, finding both balance and greater success.

Final Reflection

You can work smarter, not harder. Focus your energy on what truly drives results.

III
Relationships and Communication

At the heart of every success story, and behind each meaningful connection, lies the power of effective relationships and communication. In this section, we dive deep into the essential skills needed to connect with others authentically, navigate complex social dynamics, and foster healthier relationships. Whether it's mastering the art of influence, cultivating vulnerability and courage, or learning how to protect your emotional well-being from toxic influences, these chapters will equip you with invaluable tools for personal and professional growth. Strong relationships aren't just a nice-to-have—they're the foundation of a fulfilling, successful life.

Before beginning this section, take a few minutes to consider how you currently interact with others and the quality of your relationships. This questionnaire is designed to help you gauge your strengths and weaknesses in communication, emotional openness, and managing difficult people. Respond truthfully, and use your answers to identify where you can enhance your skills and build healthier, more fulfilling connections. Let this be a guide to deepening your relationships and improving how you engage with those around you.

Relationship and Communication Self-Assessment

Check the box next to the response that best describes your current approach to relationships and communication.

1. How do you handle conflicts in your relationships (personal or professional)?

☐ A. I communicate openly and work toward resolving conflicts constructively.

☐ B. I try to avoid conflicts but struggle with finding the best way to resolve them.

☐ C. I often avoid conflicts or feel overwhelmed, and they remain unresolved.

2. How do you express your feelings and needs to others?

☐ A. I communicate my feelings and needs clearly and respectfully.

☐ B. I communicate sometimes, but I struggle with being clear or direct.

☐ C. I rarely express my feelings or needs, and often feel misunderstood.

3. How well do you listen to others during conversations?

☐ A. I actively listen and show empathy to understand their perspective.

☐ B. I listen, but I sometimes focus more on what I'm going to say next.

☐ C. I often feel distracted or disconnected during conversations.

4. How do you feel about being vulnerable in your relationships?

☐ A. I'm comfortable with vulnerability and see it as a strength in building trust.

☐ B. I struggle with vulnerability but try to open up when necessary.

☐ C. I avoid being vulnerable because it makes me feel uncomfortable or exposed.

5. How do you manage boundaries in your relationships?

☐ A. I set and respect clear boundaries for myself and others.

☐ B. I sometimes struggle with setting or enforcing boundaries.

☐ C. I rarely set boundaries and often feel overwhelmed or taken advantage of.

6. How do you handle criticism or feedback from others?

☐ A. I accept feedback constructively and use it as an opportunity for growth.

☐ B. I take feedback seriously but sometimes feel defensive.

☐ C. I struggle to accept criticism and often feel hurt or attacked by it.

7. How do you support the people in your life?

☐ A. I actively support and encourage others, and I make time for them.

☐ B. I try to be supportive, but I sometimes find it difficult to balance my needs with others'.

☐ C. I want to be more supportive, but I often feel too overwhelmed by my own challenges.

Reflection & Next Steps

Mostly A's: You have a strong foundation in building healthy, fulfilling relationships and communicating effectively. The next section will help you deepen your connections and strengthen your communication skills even further, so you can continue growing in both personal and professional relationships.

Mostly B's: You're doing well, but there's room for improvement in how you manage your relationships and communication. The upcoming chapters will provide you with practical strategies for setting boundaries, expressing vulnerability, and handling conflicts constructively, so you can enhance your relationships and feel more confident in your interactions.

Mostly C's: It seems like you're facing some significant challenges when it comes to relationships and communication. This section will give you the tools you need to improve how you connect with others, from setting boundaries to expressing your needs, and finding healthier ways to handle conflicts. Don't worry—you're about to learn how to create meaningful, supportive relationships with greater ease.

21

The Power of People Skills

In a world that seems to be more connected than ever, ironically, many of us feel disconnected. We can get lost in screens, texts, and notifications, forgetting the essential truth that people skills are at the core of almost everything we want to achieve in life. Whether it's landing that dream job, building strong friendships, improving your relationships, or simply making your day-to-day interactions smoother and more enjoyable, mastering interpersonal skills is one of the smartest investments you can make.

Think about it: no matter how talented or knowledgeable you are, if you can't communicate effectively or build genuine connections, your abilities are limited. You might be an incredible engineer, a creative genius, or a financial wizard, but if you don't know how to work with people, you'll constantly hit walls. Your relationships—professional, personal, and everything in between—are the foundation of your success. So, let's explore how honing your interpersonal skills can transform the way you interact with the world.

Why People Skills Are the Key to Success

Imagine you're at a party or networking event, and you meet someone new. You might forget their name after the conversation ends, but you will never forget how they made you feel. That's the real magic of interpersonal skills—making people feel valued, understood, and appreciated. The ability to create positive feelings in others is what opens doors and builds lasting relationships.

Having good people skills isn't just about being likable (although that helps!); it's understanding others and being able to influence outcomes in a positive way, it's connecting authentically, making others feel important, and genuinely caring about their perspective.

Here's the kicker: people don't just want to work with smart, talented people—they want to work with those who are empathetic, kind, and easy to be around. The right skills can make you not only more successful in business but also a better friend, partner, and communicator in all areas of life.

The Foundation of Great People Skills: Empathy

At the core of strong interpersonal skills is empathy. Empathy is the ability to step into someone else's shoes and truly understand their perspective, feelings, and needs. It's the secret ingredient to forming genuine connections with others because when people feel understood, they feel seen.

Empathy can turn a simple conversation into a meaningful exchange. It's what makes people open up, trust you, and want to work with you. The best part? Empathy isn't something you're either born with or not—it's a skill you can develop. The more you practice tuning into the emotions of others, the better you get at it.

Example: Let's say you're in a work meeting, and a colleague is visibly frustrated about a project. Instead of dismissing their frustration or jumping in with your own opinion, you pause and say, "I can see you're really frustrated with how things are going. Can you walk me through what's bothering you?" Just by acknowledging their feelings and inviting them to share more, you've opened a door to understanding and connection. You've shown that you're not just listening—you're caring.

The Art of Listening: The Underrated Superpower

One of the simplest yet most overlooked aspects of strong people skills is the art of listening. Truly listening to someone is one of the most powerful ways to show them that you value and respect them. Yet, in today's fast-paced world, many of us are guilty of half-listening. We nod along while thinking about what we're going to say next or checking our phones.

Active listening is different. It's giving your full attention, putting aside distractions, and really focusing on what the other person is saying—both their words and their emotions.

How to Be a Better Listener:

Make eye contact: This shows that you're present in the conversation.

Don't interrupt: Let the person finish their thoughts before jumping in.

Summarize or reflect back: Saying something like, "So, what I'm hearing is that you're concerned about X, is that right?" shows that you're engaged and paying attention.

When you practice listening, you'll be amazed at how much more smoothly your conversations go and how much deeper your relationships become. People will notice—and they'll appreciate it more than you think.

The Power of Positive Reinforcement: Make People Feel Valued

One of the best ways to strengthen your connections with others is by making people feel valued. Everyone, deep down, wants to feel important. We all crave recognition and appreciation. So, one of the quickest ways to build rapport with someone is by offering genuine compliments and positive reinforcement.

But here's the key: it has to be genuine. People can tell when you're being insincere or giving empty flattery. Instead of focusing on surface-level compliments like "Nice shirt," dig a little deeper. Acknowledge someone's effort, dedication, or a unique quality that you truly admire.

Example: Instead of just saying, "You're really good at your job," try something more specific like, "I've noticed how detail-oriented you are, especially in those last few projects. It's really impressive how you manage to catch things that others might overlook."

This type of compliment doesn't just make the person feel good—it shows that you've taken the time to observe and appreciate them on a deeper level.

Everyone, deep down, wants to feel important. We all crave recognition and appreciation.

Influence Without Manipulation: The Win-Win Approach

There's a fine line between influence and manipulation, and the difference is intent. When you genuinely want the best for others and seek outcomes that benefit everyone, that's influence. Manipulation, on the other hand, is self-serving and often comes at the expense of others.

In any interaction, if you focus on creating a win-win situation, you're using positive influence. It's about helping people see why an idea, decision, or action benefits them, too. When you approach situations with this mindset, you're not just looking for what's in it for you—you're looking for how you can add value to the other person's life.

Example: Imagine you're trying to persuade a colleague to support your idea for a new project. Instead of framing it as, "This is what I want," you could say, "I think this project could really benefit our team by streamlining processes and saving us a lot of time in the long run. What do you think? How could we make this work for everyone?"

By framing it as something that benefits the group, not just you, you're much more likely to gain support and build goodwill in the process.

Building Trust: The Foundation of Lasting Relationships

Trust is the bedrock of all successful relationships, whether personal or professional. Without trust, there's no connection. Trust is built through honesty, reliability, and consistency. People need to know that they can count on you, that you'll keep your word, and that you'll be transparent in your actions and intentions.

How to Build Trust:

Be honest: Even when it's uncomfortable, tell the truth. People respect honesty, even when it's tough to hear.

Keep your promises: Follow through on what you say you'll do. If you commit to something, make sure it happens.

Admit mistakes: When you mess up (and we all do), own it. Apologize and make it right.

Trust takes time to build, but once it's there, it forms the foundation for all your future interactions.

How to Start Improving Your People Skills Today

Developing great interpersonal skills doesn't happen overnight, but with conscious effort, you can start seeing improvements quickly. The good news? It's something you can work on daily, in small, practical ways.

The Listening Challenge

For the next week, commit to being a better listener. In every conversation—whether with a colleague, a friend, your partner or even a stranger—make a conscious effort to listen more than you speak. Put away distractions, make eye contact, and really focus on what the other person is saying. Notice how your conversations change when you listen actively.

The Compliment Experiment

Each day, offer someone a genuine compliment. It could be about their work, their personality, or something specific you've observed. Pay attention to how people respond when you make them feel valued. Keep a journal to note the effect this has on your interactions.

Reflect and Adapt

At the end of each day, reflect on your conversations. Think about what went well and where you could improve. Did you interrupt someone without realizing it? Did you miss an opportunity to offer positive reinforcement? By reflecting regularly, you'll start becoming more aware of your habits and can consciously adapt.

▶ Immediate Action: Build Authentic Relationships with Active Engagement

Mastering people skills isn't just about being charismatic; it's about forming meaningful, genuine connections. This exercise will help you practice key interpersonal skills such as empathy, active listening, and positive reinforcement to improve your relationships—both personal and professional.

Step 1: Identify Key Relationships

Start by identifying three people in your life—these can be colleagues, friends, or family members—with whom you want to build a stronger connection. Write down their names and think about your current relationship with them. Are there areas for improvement? Could communication be smoother? Understanding where you stand is the first step toward progress.

Step 2: Practice Active Listening

For the next week, focus on active listening in every interaction with these three people. When talking to them, eliminate distractions (put down your phone, turn off your computer screen) and make a conscious effort to listen deeply. Pay attention not just to their words but also to their tone, body language, and emotions. After they've finished speaking, reflect back what you've heard by saying something like, "It sounds like you're feeling [insert emotion], is that right?" This reinforces that you're genuinely tuned in to their perspective.

Step 3: Show Empathy and Validate Their Experience

In each conversation, actively work on showing empathy by validating their emotions and experiences. For instance, if someone shares that they've been feeling stressed or overwhelmed, instead of jumping to solutions or dismissing their feelings, respond with something like, "I can understand why you'd feel that way—it sounds like you've got a lot on your plate." Empathy builds trust and helps others feel understood, which is the cornerstone of great people skills.

Step 4: Offer Genuine Positive Reinforcement

Make a habit of offering meaningful, specific compliments or feedback to the same three individuals. Instead of generic praise, focus on recognizing something unique about them. For example, "I really appreciate how you stayed calm during that meeting even when things got tense. It helped the whole team stay focused." This type of recognition makes others feel valued and encourages them to open up more in the future.

Step 5: Reflect and Adjust

At the end of each day, take a few minutes to reflect on your interactions. Ask yourself: Did I truly listen, or was I waiting to speak? Was I empathetic in my response? Did I make the person feel valued? Write down your reflections in a journal. Notice how, over time, your ability to connect with others improves as you practice these essential skills.

Step 6: Extend Beyond Your Comfort Zone

Finally, challenge yourself to apply these skills with someone outside your immediate circle—a new colleague, an acquaintance, or even a service worker. Authentic connections aren't reserved for just close friends or coworkers; they can be built anywhere. Engaging genuinely with people beyond your usual network will further strengthen your interpersonal skillset.

By committing to active listening, empathy, and positive reinforcement over time, you'll notice a significant improvement in how others respond to you. Building authentic relationships through these small but meaningful actions is the key to not only improving your communication but also unlocking new opportunities for collaboration, trust, and deeper connections across all areas of your life.

Questions for Reflection

- Think about a recent conversation where you felt genuinely connected to the other person. What people skills did you use that helped create that connection?

- In what areas of your life do you feel your people skills could be stronger? How do you think improving these skills could impact your personal or professional relationships?

- When was the last time you practiced active listening without distractions? How did it affect the quality of the conversation?

- Do you find it challenging to empathize with others when they are upset or frustrated? What could you do to practice empathy in these moments, even if you don't fully agree with their perspective?

- Consider how you handle feedback or criticism from others. Are you open to receiving it with grace, or do you tend to get defensive? How can improving your response help you grow?

- How often do you offer genuine compliments or positive reinforcement to the people around you? How does this practice influence your relationships and work environment?

- Reflect on a time when you failed to build trust with someone. What could you have done differently to cultivate a deeper sense of trust in that relationship?

Conclusion: The Power of Connection

Mastering people skills is more than just learning how to talk to others. It's connecting on a deeper level, building trust, and making people feel valued. When you invest time and effort into improving your interpersonal skills, you'll not only see a huge difference in your personal and professional life but also in how much more fulfilling your relationships become.

Success in life is rarely achieved in isolation. Whether you're working on a team, building a business, or nurturing personal relationships, the ability to connect with and influence others is your greatest asset. So, start today. Focus on empathy, listening, and trust-building. Every small improvement will have a ripple effect on the world around you.

Success is built on the relationships you create. Cultivate them wisely, and you'll find that people are your greatest allies in achieving your goals.

Final Reflection

True connection happens when we step outside of ourselves and fully engage with others.

22

Four Simple Principles to Live a Free and Happy Life

Have you ever felt like you're trapped in your own mind? Like there's a constant stream of pressure, expectations, and worries clouding your happiness and sense of freedom? You're not alone. Many of us carry the weight of unnecessary stress, self-doubt, and fear because of how we've been conditioned to think and behave. But what if I told you that there's a simple way to break free? That by following four straightforward principles, you could let go of this emotional baggage and experience a deeper sense of freedom and happiness?

In this chapter, we're going to dive into these four guiding principles that, if practiced consistently, can dramatically transform how you live your life. These aren't complicated strategies or life hacks—just simple agreements you make with yourself to live with more awareness, peace, and purpose. So, let's get started.

Be Spotless with Your Words: Speak with Integrity

Words have immense power. They shape how we see ourselves and others, influence our emotions, and even determine the course of our lives. When you speak with honesty, integrity, and kindness, you're creating a positive environment not only for yourself but for those around you. On the flip side, when you speak carelessly, gossip, or use words to harm, you invite negativity into your life.

Think of your words as seeds. What you plant in the world—whether positive or negative—grows. If you constantly criticize yourself or others, you're cultivating a world full of negativity. If you choose to use your words for encouragement, truth, and kindness, you'll build a garden of positivity that benefits everyone.

How to Practice It:

Start with yourself. How do you talk to yourself? When you make a mistake, are you harsh and judgmental? Practice being kind and encouraging in your self-talk. It might feel strange at first, but over time, this shift in language can boost your confidence and happiness.

Avoid gossip. It's tempting to vent about someone when they're not around, but gossip always comes back to bite you. When you catch yourself about to talk negatively about someone, pause. Ask yourself: is this necessary? What's my intention?

Example: Let's say you've had a tough day at home, and your first instinct is to complain to a friend about how annoying your partner was. Instead of diving into negativity, flip the narrative. You might say, "Today was tough, but I'm grateful I kept my cool in a stressful situation." This small shift keeps the conversation positive and helps you stay in control of your emotional state.

Don't Take Anything on a Personal Level: It's Not About You

One of the biggest sources of unhappiness is the habit of taking things personally. Someone cuts you off in traffic, and you immediately think, "Why is everyone so rude to me?" Your boss gives you critical feedback, and you start questioning your abilities. But here's the truth: what people say or do is usually a reflection of them, not you.

Everyone is living their own story, shaped by their beliefs, experiences, and emotions. When someone lashes out or criticizes you, it's often because of their own struggles, fears, or misunderstandings. When you stop taking things personally, you free yourself from unnecessary suffering.

How to Practice It:

Pause before reacting. When someone says something that feels hurtful, take a deep breath and remind yourself that their words or actions are a reflection of them, not you.

Don't seek validation. Your worth doesn't depend on others' opinions. You don't need everyone to like or approve of you. Trust in your own values and let go of the need for external validation.

What people say or do is usually a reflection of them, not you.

Example: Imagine you're at a family gathering, and a relative makes a snarky comment about your life choices. Instead of letting it ruin your mood, recognize that their opinion is based on their perspective—not a reflection of your worth or the validity of your decisions. You might respond with a neutral comment like, "That's an interesting point of view," and move on. No emotional energy wasted!

Don't Make Suppositions: Ask for Clarity

We've all been guilty of jumping to conclusions. We assume we know what someone else is thinking or why they're acting a certain way, and then we react based on those assumptions. The problem? Most of the time, we're wrong. Assumptions create misunderstandings, unnecessary drama, and hurt feelings.

Instead of assuming, ask questions. Clarify what someone meant. Seek to understand before reacting. You'd be amazed at how many conflicts could be avoided if people just asked, "What did you mean by that?" instead of assuming the worst.

How to Practice It:

Ask for clarification. When you're unsure about what someone is saying or thinking, don't fill in the blanks with your assumptions. Simply ask. "Can you explain what you meant by that?" goes a long way in avoiding confusion.

Challenge your assumptions. When you catch yourself making assumptions (e.g., "She didn't respond to my text because she's mad at me"), take a step back. Ask yourself if there's another possible explanation.

Example: You text a friend, and they don't reply for hours. Instead of assuming they're ignoring you or upset, remind yourself that they could be busy or dealing with something unrelated to you. When you next speak, instead of saying, "Why didn't you respond?" you could say, "Hey, just wanted to check if everything's okay. I noticed you didn't reply earlier."

Always Do the Best You Can: No Regrets, Just Growth

Life is not about being perfect—it's about doing your best with what you have in the moment. Some days, your best might look like tackling a huge project at work with energy and focus. Other days, your best might be simply getting out of bed and taking care of yourself. And that's okay.

When you commit to always doing your best, you eliminate regret. You can look back at your day or your life knowing you gave it your all, even if things didn't turn out perfectly. Doing your best doesn't mean striving for perfection—it means putting forth your best effort, whatever that looks like today.

How to Practice It:

Set realistic expectations. Your best changes depending on circumstances. Don't hold yourself to impossible standards. Aim to improve, but also be kind to yourself on tough days.

Learn from mistakes. When things don't go as planned, instead of beating yourself up, ask yourself: "What can I learn from this?" Growth comes from reflection, not self-criticism.

Example: You have a presentation at work, and you spend hours preparing. On the day of, your nerves get the best of you, and it doesn't go as smoothly as you hoped. Instead of dwelling on what went wrong, focus on the fact that you gave it your best shot. Then, ask yourself: "What can I do differently next time to feel more confident?" Growth is a journey, not a destination.

Practical Exercises for Everyday Life

Now that you understand these four simple agreements, it's time to put them into action. The key is practice. These principles aren't one-and-done; they require daily awareness and effort. Here are some exercises to help you integrate them into your life:

Mindful Speech Challenge

For the next week, commit to being mindful of every word you speak. Before you say something, ask yourself: Is it true? Is it kind? Is it necessary? Track how your interactions change when you focus on speaking with integrity.

Let It Go Practice

Every time you catch yourself taking something personally, stop. Take a deep breath and remind yourself that it's not about you. Notice how much lighter you feel when you don't take things to heart.

Clarity Conversations

Pick one situation where you've made an assumption—about a friend, colleague, or family member. Instead of assuming, ask for clarification. Approach the conversation with curiosity and a desire to understand, rather than assuming you know the whole story.

Do Your Best, Reflect, Repeat

At the end of each day, take five minutes to reflect. Ask yourself: Did I do my best today? What did I learn? If there's something you wish you'd done differently, make a mental note to apply that lesson tomorrow. This daily reflection will help you grow without regret.

▶ Immediate Action: Letting Go of Emotional Baggage

To truly live a free and happy life, it's essential to recognize and release the emotional burdens that weigh you down. This exercise will guide you in identifying and letting go of unnecessary attachments, allowing for greater peace and joy.

Identify Your Burdens: Take a moment to reflect on what's currently weighing on your mind. It could be a past mistake, a toxic relationship, or unresolved conflict. Write down at least three specific things that you feel are holding you back from experiencing happiness and freedom.

Evaluate the Impact: For each burden you've listed, ask yourself: How does this make me feel? How is it affecting my daily life, relationships, or overall happiness? Write a few sentences about the negative impact these burdens have on your life. This step is crucial for recognizing the true cost of holding onto these feelings.

Choose to Release: After identifying and evaluating your burdens, it's time to let them go. Take a piece of paper and write down a powerful statement for each burden that encapsulates your decision to release it. For example: "I choose to let go of my fear of failure and embrace growth."

Create a Ritual of Release: Find a meaningful way to symbolize your release. This could be as simple as tearing the paper into pieces, burning it safely, or even letting it drift away in a body of water. As you perform this ritual, visualize yourself freeing your mind and heart from the emotional baggage, feeling lighter and more liberated with each action.

Reflect on Your Freedom: After the ritual, take a few moments to sit quietly and reflect on how it feels to release these burdens. Journal your thoughts about the experience. How does it feel to let go? What do you want to invite into your life now that you have released these weights? This reflection will help solidify your commitment to living freely and happily.

By consciously engaging in this exercise, you create space for happiness and allow yourself to embrace the freedom that comes from letting go of the past. Remember, true freedom is not about never feeling burdened; it's about choosing to release what no longer serves you and moving forward with intention and purpose.

Questions for Reflection

- How do the four principles resonate with your current mindset and behaviors? Which principle do you find most challenging to embrace?

- In what ways have your words—both to yourself and others—shaped your reality? Can you identify a recent situation where your language influenced the outcome?

- Think about a recent experience where you took something personally. How might your perspective shift if you recognized that it was more about the other person's struggles than your own worth?

- Reflect on a time you made an assumption about someone's intentions. How did that assumption impact your relationship? What could you have done differently to foster understanding?

- What actions can you take today to ensure you are always doing your best? How will you measure your personal growth moving forward?

Conclusion: The Path to Freedom and Happiness

Living by these four simple principles can have a profound impact on your life. You'll find a greater sense of freedom, peace, and happiness.

These agreements are tools. The more you use them, the more natural they'll become, and over time, you'll notice that life feels lighter, smoother, and more fulfilling. So, start today. Commit to these principles, and watch as they unlock new levels of personal freedom and happiness in your lif

Final Reflection

Your happiness is a choice, not a reaction to others.

23

Vulnerability: Living with Courage and Authenticity

Have you ever felt the need to hide parts of who you are because you're afraid of what others might think? Maybe you've held back from sharing your true feelings, or you've avoided taking a risk because the fear of failure was too overwhelming. We've all been there. We live in a world that often tells us to keep it together, be strong, and never show weakness. But what if I told you that the very thing we're taught to avoid—vulnerability—is actually the key to living a courageous and authentic life?

Let's explore the true meaning of vulnerability, why it's so important, and how embracing it can unlock a life full of connection, joy, and bravery. Vulnerability is not exposing your deepest secrets or being weak. Vulnerability is showing up as your true self, even when it's uncomfortable or scary, and that is where real courage begins.

What Is Vulnerability, Really?

Let's start by clearing up a common misconception: vulnerability isn't being fragile or helpless or airing your every insecurity or being open to getting hurt. In fact, vulnerability is one of the most courageous things you can do. It's about risking emotional exposure, letting others see the real you, and accepting the uncertainty of life.

Think about it: Every time you open up to someone, admit that you don't have all the answers, or take a chance on something important to you, you're being vulnerable. And it's not easy. We fear being judged, rejected, or seen as weak. But here's the truth—without vulnerability, there is no real connection. Without vulnerability, we can't experience true intimacy, joy, or personal growth.

So, if you want to live authentically and courageously, you need to lean into vulnerability.

Why Do We Avoid Vulnerability?

The fear of vulnerability comes from a deep-rooted belief that showing our true selves—our flaws, our struggles, our dreams—makes us less worthy of love and acceptance. Society tells us to be perfect, to have it all together. As a result, many of us wear masks, hiding the parts of ourselves we think others won't accept.

Without vulnerability, there is no real connection.

The problem with this? It's exhausting. It takes so much energy to constantly pretend that everything's fine when inside, you're feeling anxious, uncertain, or imperfect. And it creates distance between us and the people who matter most. When you're always trying to be perfect, you miss out on opportunities for genuine connection.

Let's face it, life is messy. We all have moments of doubt, failure, and uncertainty. By pretending otherwise, we rob ourselves of the chance to experience true courage and authenticity.

The Link Between Vulnerability and Courage

Here's the game-changer: vulnerability and courage are inseparable. You can't have one without the other. Think about any time you've had to do something brave—whether it was speaking up in a meeting, starting a new project, or expressing your true feelings to someone. In those moments, you were vulnerable. You didn't know how things would turn out, but you went for it anyway.

That's what courage is—taking action despite uncertainty. And vulnerability is the space where courage happens.

When we embrace vulnerability, we're saying, "I'm willing to be seen. I'm willing to take risks. I'm willing to be imperfect." That's a bold move. And it's the foundation of living a wholehearted, authentic life.

The Benefits of Embracing Vulnerability

You might still be thinking, "Okay, I get it, but why would I willingly make myself vulnerable?" Good question. Here's why vulnerability is worth it:

Deeper Connections: Vulnerability creates real connections with others. When you open up and share your true self, you invite others to do the same. This builds trust, intimacy, and stronger relationships.

Increased Resilience: When you stop trying to be perfect, you build emotional resilience. You become more comfortable with failure and uncertainty, which allows you to bounce back more quickly when things don't go as planned.

Greater Creativity and Innovation: Taking risks and being open to failure fuels creativity and innovation. Many breakthroughs come from the willingness to try something new, even if it might not work.

More Authenticity: Vulnerability helps you live more authentically. When you're not worried about being perfect, you can show up as the real you—flaws and all. This authenticity attracts the right people and opportunities into your life.

Less Stress: Letting go of the need to control everything reduces stress and anxiety. Vulnerability helps you accept that life is uncertain and that's okay.

How to Practice Vulnerability

Now that we've covered why vulnerability is so important, let's talk about how to actually put it into practice. Being vulnerable isn't something that happens overnight, but with small, consistent efforts, you can become more comfortable embracing it in your everyday life.

Start Small: You don't have to dive into deep vulnerability right away. Start by sharing something a little personal with someone you trust—a fear, a hope, or a story about a challenge you've faced. The more you practice opening up, the more natural it will feel.

Let Go of Perfection: Perfectionism is the enemy of vulnerability. When you're always trying to be perfect, you avoid risks and the possibility of failure. Instead, focus on progress, not perfection. Be willing to make mistakes and learn from them.

Be Kind to Yourself: Self-compassion is key to vulnerability. When you're kind to yourself, you create a safe space to be imperfect and make mistakes. Instead of beating yourself up for not having it all figured out, remind yourself that you're doing your best, and that's enough.

Embrace Uncertainty: Life is full of uncertainty, and that's okay. When you accept that you can't control everything, you allow yourself to take risks and step into the unknown. This is where growth happens. The next time you feel unsure, instead of retreating, lean into it. Trust that you'll figure it out as you go.

Ask for Help: A big part of vulnerability is admitting when you need help. Whether it's reaching out to a friend for support or asking a colleague for advice, letting others in shows strength, not weakness. It also deepens your relationships.

Examples of Vulnerability in Action

Let's take a look at a few examples of how vulnerability can show up in everyday life:

At Work: You're in a meeting, and there's something you don't fully understand. Instead of pretending you get it, you raise your hand

and ask for clarification. This simple act of vulnerability shows courage and can actually earn you more respect from your colleagues.

In Relationships: You've been feeling distant from a close friend. Instead of keeping your feelings bottled up, you have an honest conversation, sharing how you've been feeling and asking if they've noticed the same thing. This kind of vulnerability can lead to a deeper connection and understanding.

In Creativity: You've been working on a personal project, like writing or painting, but you're scared of showing it to others because it's not "perfect" yet. Vulnerability means sharing it anyway, knowing that it may not be perfect but still having the courage to put yourself out there.

Practical Exercises: Building Your Vulnerability Muscles

Here are some exercises you can do to start embracing vulnerability in your life:

Vulnerability Journal

At the end of each day, write down one moment where you allowed yourself to be vulnerable. Maybe it was asking for help, sharing your feelings, or admitting you didn't know something. Reflect on how it felt and what you learned from the experience.

Reach Out

Think of someone you've been meaning to connect with but have been holding back for fear of rejection or judgment. Reach out to them. Send a message, ask them how they're doing, or set up a time to meet. Opening that door is a vulnerable act, but it's also a brave one.

Share Something Real

The next time someone asks how you're doing, be honest. Instead of saying, "I'm fine," share a real emotion or experience you've been going through. It doesn't have to be deeply personal, but start practicing authenticity in small conversations.

Challenge Perfectionism

Pick one area of your life where you've been striving for perfection. It could be at work, in a hobby, or in your appearance. Set a goal to take one action where you allow yourself to be imperfect. For example, submit a project that's "good enough" instead of perfect, or post a picture without editing it. Notice how it feels to let go of the pressure to be flawless.

▶ Immediate Action: Open Up to Someone

To embrace the power of vulnerability, commit to sharing a piece of your true self with someone you trust. This immediate action is about taking a courageous step toward authentic connection and personal growth.

Choose Your Person: Think of someone in your life—a friend, family member, or colleague—whom you feel safe with. This should be someone who supports you and is likely to respond with kindness.

Select a Topic: Identify a specific aspect of your life that you want to share. It could be a fear you've been holding onto, a personal goal, or even a recent struggle. Aim for something that feels meaningful but is manageable for you to discuss.

Prepare Your Thoughts: Before the conversation, take a moment to jot down your thoughts or feelings. How does this topic impact you? What emotions are tied to it? This preparation will help you articulate your feelings more clearly when you speak.

Have the Conversation: Initiate a conversation with your chosen person. You might say something like, "I've been wanting to share something personal with you that's been on my mind." Open up about the topic you selected, allowing yourself to be honest and vulnerable.

Reflect on the Experience: After the conversation, take a moment to reflect. How did it feel to share? Were there any surprises in how the other person reacted? Write down your thoughts in a journal, noting the emotions that arose during the conversation and how you felt afterward.

This exercise fosters connection with others and also strengthens your ability to be vulnerable, paving the way for deeper relationships and a more authentic life. Every act of vulnerability is a step toward living with greater courage.

Questions for Reflection

- What moments in my life have I avoided vulnerability, and what impact has that had on my relationships and sense of self?

- How do I typically react when I feel vulnerable, and what can I learn from those reactions?

- In what areas of my life am I holding back due to fear of judgment or rejection?

- What small steps can I take to embrace vulnerability in my daily interactions?

- How can I foster a safe space for others to be vulnerable around me?

Conclusion: The Courage to Be Vulnerable

Embracing vulnerability isn't being weak or oversharing; it's having the courage to show up fully in your life. When you let down your walls and let others see the real you, you create space for connection, growth, and joy. Living authentically takes practice, but the rewards are totally worth it.

Vulnerability is a strength, not a weakness. It's the doorway to living a brave and wholehearted life. So, take a deep breath, step into the discomfort, and trust that being vulnerable is the bravest thing you can do. Because it is.

Final Reflection

Daring to be seen can transform not only your own life but also the lives of those around you.

24
Identifying and Distancing Yourself from Toxic People

We've all encountered people who leave us feeling drained, upset, or even questioning our self-worth after interacting with them. These individuals might be friends, coworkers, or even family members. But no matter who they are, they have one thing in common: they create negativity in our lives, often without us even realizing how much harm they're causing. These are toxic people, and learning to identify and distance yourself from them is key to protecting your mental and emotional well-being.

Now we'll dive into the signs of toxic behavior, why it's so important to set boundaries with these individuals, and how you can take control of your relationships to create a more positive and supportive environment for yourself. By the end, you'll feel empowered to prioritize your well-being and make healthier choices when it comes to the people you surround yourself with.

What Is a Toxic Person?

Let's start by clarifying what we mean by a toxic person. Toxic people aren't necessarily bad people, but they have behaviors that are harmful to those around them. Whether it's through manipulation, constant negativity, or emotional draining, their behavior affects your mental health, self-esteem, and happiness. Toxic individuals can be subtle in how they undermine you, or they can be overt, but the end result is the same: they leave you feeling worse off after interacting with them.

Here are some common traits of toxic people:

- **Chronic Negativity**: They always see the glass as half-empty and tend to complain about everything. No matter how positive you try to be, they'll drag the mood down.

- **Drama and Chaos**: Toxic people thrive on drama. They stir up conflict, either in their own lives or in yours, and seem to always be in the middle of a crisis.

- **Manipulation**: They use guilt, fear, or emotional tactics to get what they want, often making you feel like you owe them something or that their needs should come first.

- **Lack of Accountability**: Toxic individuals never take responsibility for their actions. If something goes wrong, it's always someone else's fault—often yours.

- **Inconsistent Behavior**: One minute they're supportive, the next they're tearing you down. This inconsistency keeps you guessing and walking on eggshells around them.

- **Criticism and Judgment**: They're quick to criticize and make you feel like you're not enough. Whether it's direct or subtle, they constantly find ways to put you down.

Toxic people leave you feeling worse off after interacting with them.

Why Toxic People Are Harmful to Your Well-being

Spending time around toxic individuals can have a serious impact on your mental health, self-esteem, and overall sense of peace. Here's why:

- **Emotional Drain**: Toxic people drain your emotional energy. After spending time with them, you might feel exhausted, stressed, or anxious. This emotional toll can leave you feeling like you're constantly on edge or depleted.

- **Self-Doubt**: Toxic individuals often chip away at your confidence by constantly criticizing or undermining you. Over time, this can make you question your self-worth and abilities.

- **Lost Time and Energy**: When you're caught up in the chaos and emotional rollercoaster of a toxic relationship, it can distract you from focusing on what truly matters—your goals, happiness, and well-being.

- **Increased Stress**: Whether it's dealing with their drama, negativity, or manipulation, toxic people create stress in your life. This can lead to anxiety, sleepless nights, and even physical health issues like headaches or fatigue.

Recognizing these effects is the first step toward making a change. You deserve relationships that uplift and support you, not ones that pull you down.

How to Identify Toxic People in Your Life

So, how do you know if someone in your life is toxic? Here are a few questions to ask yourself when evaluating a relationship:

Do I feel worse after spending time with this person? If every interaction leaves you feeling drained, frustrated, or anxious, this is a red flag.

Do they respect my boundaries? Toxic people often push boundaries, making you feel guilty or uncomfortable when you try to assert your needs.

Are they supportive of my goals and happiness? A healthy relationship is one where both people support each other's growth. If someone is always putting you down or dismissing your dreams, they may be toxic.

Do they create unnecessary drama? If they seem to always be at the center of a crisis or thrive on stirring up conflict, this is a sign of toxicity.

Do they take responsibility for their actions? Toxic people rarely admit they're wrong and often deflect blame onto others.

If you answered "yes" to several of these questions, it's likely that you're dealing with a toxic individual.

How to Distance Yourself from Toxic People

Now that you've identified the toxic people in your life, how do you go about creating distance? It's not always easy, especially if the person is a close friend, family member, or coworker. But distancing yourself is essential for protecting your mental and emotional health.

Set Clear Boundaries. The first step in dealing with a toxic person is setting clear boundaries. Toxic individuals often push limits and expect you to tolerate their behavior. Establishing boundaries means letting them know what's acceptable and what's not—and sticking to it. For example, if a friend is constantly dumping their negativity on you, let them know that you're happy to support them but can't engage in endless complaining.

Example: "I understand you're going through a tough time, but I need us to focus on finding solutions instead of just talking about the problems."

Limit Contact. In some cases, reducing the amount of time you spend with a toxic person can significantly improve your well-being. This doesn't mean you have to cut them out completely (although, in some cases, that might be necessary), but limiting contact can give you the emotional space you need.

If it's someone you see regularly—like a coworker—try to minimize interactions to what's strictly necessary. If it's a friend or family member, limit social gatherings or phone calls to times when you feel strong enough to handle them.

Don't Engage in Their Drama. Toxic people often thrive on drama and conflict. They may try to pull you into their problems or create tension just for the sake of it. One of the best ways to protect yourself is by refusing to engage in the drama. Stay calm, avoid getting defensive, and don't let them push your buttons.

Example: If a toxic friend starts stirring up trouble, you can say something like, "I don't think it's helpful to get involved in this situation. Let's focus on something positive instead."

Be Prepared for Pushback. Toxic people don't always take kindly to boundaries or distance. They might try to guilt you, manipulate you, or even escalate their toxic behavior to keep you engaged. Stay firm. Remember, this is about protecting your well-being, and you don't owe anyone an explanation for prioritizing your health.

Example: If they accuse you of being selfish for setting boundaries, you can respond calmly: "I'm sorry you feel that way, but this is what I need to do to take care of myself right now."

Know When to Walk Away. In some cases, the best solution is to cut ties completely. If someone's toxicity is causing significant harm to your mental health or life, it might be time to end the relationship. This can be difficult, especially if it's someone close to you, but your well-being has to come first.

Practical Exercises: Protecting Your Well-being from Toxicity

Now that you understand how to identify and distance yourself from toxic people, let's put it into practice. Here are some exercises to help you strengthen your boundaries and protect your emotional well-being.

Toxicity Audit

Make a list of the people you spend the most time with—friends, family members, coworkers. For each person, reflect on how you feel after spending time with them. Do you feel uplifted and supported, or drained and anxious? This exercise will help you identify any toxic relationships you might need to address.

Set a Boundary

Think about one person in your life who frequently pushes your boundaries. What's one boundary you can set to protect your well-being? Write down how you will communicate this boundary in a calm, clear way. Practice saying it out loud so you feel confident when the time comes.

Example: "I really value our friendship, but I need to take a step back when conversations become too negative. Let's try to keep things more positive."

Create a "No-Drama" Zone

Identify one situation where you often get pulled into someone else's drama. Commit to creating a "no-drama" zone by refusing to engage in the negativity. Write down how you'll respond the next time drama arises.

Example: "If they start talking about this issue again, I'll calmly change the subject and avoid getting sucked in."

Visualize Your Support System

Spend a few minutes visualizing the people in your life who bring positivity, support, and love. Focus on how these relationships make you feel. This exercise will help you appreciate the healthy relationships in your life and remind you that you deserve connections that uplift you.

▶ Immediate Action: Create a Toxicity Awareness Plan

Navigating relationships with toxic individuals can be challenging, but creating a structured plan can empower you to reclaim your peace and well-being. This exercise will help you identify toxic dynamics, set healthy boundaries, and take action to protect your emotional health.

Step 1: Conduct a Toxicity Inventory

Begin by reflecting on the relationships in your life. Create a list of the people you interact with regularly—friends, family, colleagues, and acquaintances. Next to each name, jot down your feelings after spending time with them. Ask yourself:

- Do I feel uplifted or drained after our interactions?
- Do they respect my boundaries and support my goals?
- Do I find myself constantly involved in their drama?

This inventory will help you visualize who in your life may be toxic, allowing you to identify patterns in your emotional responses.

Step 2: Prioritize Your Relationships

Once you've completed your inventory, categorize your relationships into three groups:

- Supportive: Those who uplift and inspire you.
- Neutral: Those with whom your feelings are mixed.
- Toxic: Those who leave you feeling drained, anxious, or undermined.

Focus on nurturing the supportive relationships while developing strategies to manage or distance yourself from the toxic ones. This prioritization will help clarify where you need to set boundaries.

Step 3: Develop Boundaries

For each toxic person identified, outline specific boundaries you need to establish. This could include limiting interactions, steering conversations away from negativity, or directly communicating your needs. Write down how you plan to communicate these boundaries. For example:

"I need to limit our conversations to positive topics as I find negativity draining."

"I can't participate in discussions that involve gossip or drama."

Practicing these statements beforehand will help you feel more confident when you need to enforce these boundaries.

Step 4: Practice Self-Care

Engaging with toxic individuals can take a toll on your emotional health. Develop a self-care plan to help you recharge. This could include:

- Engaging in activities that bring you joy (hobbies, exercise, meditation).

- Setting aside time each week for reflection and journaling about your experiences.

- Reaching out to supportive friends or family to share your feelings and experiences.

- Make self-care a priority, especially after interactions with toxic people, to help mitigate their impact on your well-being.

Step 5: Implement and Reflect

Over the next few weeks, implement your Toxicity Awareness Plan. Start by applying your boundaries and engaging in self-care strategies. After each interaction with a toxic person, take a moment to reflect on how it went. Ask yourself:

- Did I feel empowered in setting my boundaries?

- How did the interaction affect my emotions and energy?

- What can I learn from this experience for future interactions?

Document your reflections in your journal to track your progress. This ongoing reflection will help you adapt your strategies as needed and reinforce your commitment to protecting your well-being.

Questions for Reflection

- Reflect on your current relationships. Are there individuals who consistently drain your energy or negatively impact your self-worth? How do you feel after interacting with them?

- Have you set clear boundaries with those who exhibit toxic behavior in your life? What specific boundaries can you establish to protect your well-being?

- Who are the people in your life that uplift and support you? How can you strengthen these relationships to create a more positive environment?

- How does being around toxic individuals affect your mental health and daily life? Are there specific behaviors that trigger stress or anxiety in these interactions?

- What immediate actions can you take to distance yourself from toxic people? Are there specific situations or interactions you can avoid in the future?

Conclusion: Taking Charge of Your Relationships

Surrounding yourself with positive, supportive people is one of the best things you can do for your mental and emotional well-being. Identifying and distancing yourself from toxic individuals isn't about being harsh or judgmental—it's about protecting your peace, your energy,

Final Reflection

As you navigate your relationships you have the power to choose who you allow into your life. Embrace that power, and prioritize your well-being above all.

IV
Spirituality and Wellness

In a world that is ever-changing and often unpredictable, the connection between spirituality and well-being becomes increasingly vital. This section invites you to explore various dimensions of spirituality that can enhance your mental, emotional, and spiritual health. Each chapter serves as a guide to help you embrace change, find fulfillment, and recognize the treasure within yourself. You'll embark on a journey that emphasizes the importance of spiritual principles for success, the healing and transformative power of your mind, and the joy that can be found in everyday moments. As you delve into the depths of self-discovery and personal growth, you will uncover the profound freedom that comes from nurturing your spirit. Prepare to embark on a path that not only enriches your life but also fosters resilience and a deep sense of purpose in an ever-evolving world.

The next questionnaire is designed to help you reflect on your spiritual journey and evaluate how it influences your overall well-being. Spirituality often encompasses a wide range of beliefs, practices, and experiences that contribute to our sense of purpose, connection, and inner peace. By taking a moment to assess your spiritual life, you can gain valuable insights into how it impacts your emotional, mental, and physical health. This self-assessment will guide you in identifying areas of strength and opportunities for growth, ultimately empowering you to cultivate a more fulfilling and balanced life. Embrace this opportunity for reflection and let it pave the way for deeper self-discovery and enhanced well-being.

Spirituality and Well-being Self-Assessment

Check the box next to the response that best describes your current approach to spirituality and well-being.

1. How often do you engage in activities that promote your spiritual well-being (e.g., meditation, prayer, or mindfulness)?

☐ A. I regularly practice spiritual activities and feel connected to my inner self.

☐ B. I occasionally engage in spiritual activities but could do more.

☐ C. I rarely participate in spiritual activities and often feel disconnected.

2. How do you handle stress and adversity in your life?

☐ A. I use positive coping strategies and seek spiritual guidance to navigate challenges.

☐ B. I try to manage stress but often feel overwhelmed and unsure how to cope.

☐ C. I struggle to handle stress and often feel lost or hopeless in tough times.

3. How connected do you feel to the world around you?

☐ A. I feel a strong connection to nature, others, and the universe.

☐ B. I sometimes feel connected, but I often lose that sense.

☐ C. I rarely feel connected and often feel isolated.

4. How often do you reflect on your values and beliefs?

☐ A. I regularly reflect on my values and strive to live in alignment with them.

☐ B. I think about my values occasionally but don't always act on them.

☐ C. I rarely reflect on my values and feel uncertain about what I truly believe.

5. How do you prioritize your mental and emotional well-being?

☐ A. I actively prioritize my mental health and seek practices that nurture my well-being.

☐ B. I try to prioritize my mental health but struggle with consistency.

☐ C. I often neglect my mental and emotional well-being and feel the effects.

6. How open are you to exploring new spiritual practices or beliefs?

☐ A. I'm very open and enjoy discovering new spiritual paths and ideas.

☐ B. I'm somewhat open but can be hesitant about trying new things.

☐ C. I'm resistant to exploring new practices and prefer to stick with what I know.

7. How well do you integrate self-care into your routine?

☐ A. I consistently practice self-care and make it a priority in my life.

☐ B. I incorporate self-care sometimes, but it's not a regular habit.

☐ C. I rarely focus on self-care and often feel drained and overwhelmed.

Reflection & Next Steps

Mostly A's: You have a solid foundation in your spiritual and emotional well-being. The upcoming chapters will enhance your existing practices, helping you deepen your connection with yourself and the universe, and continue fostering a balanced, fulfilling life.

Mostly B's: You're doing well, but there's potential for growth in your spiritual and well-being practices. This section will provide valuable insights and techniques to help you integrate more self-care, reflection, and spiritual exploration into your life, allowing you to cultivate a deeper sense of peace and fulfillment.

Mostly C's: It seems you may be facing challenges in your spiritual and emotional well-being. This section will offer tools and strategies to help you reconnect with yourself, explore new practices, and prioritize your mental health. By engaging with the material, you'll be on a path to a more balanced and harmonious life.

25

Embrace Change to Thrive in a Constantly Evolving World

Change—it's one of those things we all know is inevitable, yet it can still throw us off balance when it happens. Whether it's losing a job, a shift in a relationship, or simply the world moving faster than we can keep up with, change can feel overwhelming. But here's the thing: it's not the change itself that's the problem. The real challenge is how we react to it.

Let's see why learning to adapt to change is crucial for success and happiness. The world around us is always evolving, and those who can embrace this reality and adjust their mindset will find themselves thriving instead of struggling. And don't worry—I'll give you practical tips and exercises to help you get comfortable with change and even look forward to it.

Why Is Change So Hard?

Before we get into how to adapt to change, let's talk about why it feels so difficult in the first place. The human brain is wired for predictability and comfort. We like routines. We like knowing what's coming next. When something shifts—especially when it's unexpected—our natural instinct is to resist. Why? Because we equate change with risk. And risk, to our brains, equals danger.

When things change, whether it's a minor inconvenience like a favorite café closing or a major life shift like moving to a new city, we lose that sense of control. And as soon as we lose control, our fear of the unknown kicks in.

But here's the catch: life is all about change. No matter how much we try to cling to stability, things will always be in flux. Jobs evolve, technology advances, people come and go from our lives. Resisting change is like trying to swim upstream in a fast-flowing river—it's exhausting, and you're more likely to be swept away by the current than if you simply allowed yourself to go with the flow.

The Power of Adaptability

So, if change is inevitable, what's the solution? Adaptability. The people who succeed and thrive in life are not the ones who avoid change but the ones who learn to embrace it. They see change not as a threat, but as an opportunity.

Think of any major success story—be it in business, personal development, or even sports—and you'll see a pattern. Successful people don't fear change; they use it to their advantage. They're always thinking about how to pivot, how to adjust their strategies, and how to make the most of whatever situation they find themselves in.

> *Successful people don't fear change; they use it to their advantage.*

For example, consider the rise of remote work in recent years. Many companies that were previously office-based had to make a sudden and dramatic shift to working from home. The ones that adapted quickly found new ways to collaborate, innovate, and even grow. On the flip side, businesses that resisted the change struggled, losing both talent and opportunities.

The lesson? Those who adapt, thrive. Those who don't, get left behind.

Steps to Embrace Change

So how do we get better at adapting to change? It's a mindset shift, for sure, but it's also something you can practice. Let's break it down into steps that will help you embrace change and start seeing it as a positive force in your life.

Accept That Change Is Constant. The first step is recognizing that change is not a one-time event—it's an ongoing part of life. Instead of waiting for things to "go back to normal" or expecting stability around every corner, remind yourself that normal is constantly evolving.

A helpful way to think about this is to see life as a series of chapters. Just like in a book, each chapter is different, but they all contribute to the larger story. The chapter you're in right now may feel challenging, but it's only temporary. A new chapter is just around the corner, and it could bring incredible opportunities you never saw coming.

Shift Your Perspective. Rather than seeing change as something that's happening to you, try to see it as something that's happening for you. Ask yourself: "How can I use this change to my advantage?" or "What's the opportunity here that I might not be seeing?"

For instance, if you lose your job, instead of immediately spiraling into panic, think about it as a chance to pursue a career path you've always been curious about or to develop a new skill. Shifting your perspective can make a world of difference.

Focus on What You Can Control. One of the reasons change feels so scary is because it often comes with a lot of uncertainty. But here's the thing: you don't need to control everything. You only need to focus on what's within your power to influence.

When change happens, ask yourself: "What part of this situation can I control?" It could be how you respond emotionally, how you choose to spend your time, or even how you communicate with others. By focusing on what you can control, you'll feel more empowered and less overwhelmed.

Stay Curious. Curiosity is one of the best tools for adapting to change. Instead of jumping to conclusions or making assumptions, approach new situations with a sense of curiosity. Ask questions like, "What can I learn from this?" or "How can this experience help me grow?"

When we stay curious, we open ourselves up to possibilities we might have missed if we were too busy resisting or complaining about the change.

Build Resilience Through Small Changes. If big changes feel overwhelming, start with small ones. Practice adapting by making little tweaks to your routine or trying new things in low-stakes situations. The more you expose yourself to small, manageable changes, the more comfortable you'll become with the bigger ones.

For example, you could take a different route to work, learn a new hobby, or rearrange your furniture. These small adjustments help you flex your adaptability muscles so that when bigger changes come along, you're better prepared.

Exercises for Adapting to Change

Let's put this into practice. Here are some exercises to help you get comfortable with change and build resilience.

Change Audit

Make a list of recent changes in your life, both big and small. For each one, write down how you initially reacted to the change and what the outcome was. Then, ask yourself: How could I have approached this change differently? What could I have learned from it? This exercise helps you reflect on your relationship with change and identify areas where you can improve.

Reframe a Current Challenge

Think about a change or challenge you're currently facing. Write down all the negative thoughts you have about it. Then, take each of those negative thoughts and reframe them into something positive. For example:

Negative: "I'm overwhelmed by all the new responsibilities at work."

Positive: "This is a chance for me to grow my skills and show what I'm capable of."

This exercise helps shift your mindset from one of resistance to one of opportunity.

Plan for Future Changes

Think about areas of your life where change is likely to occur in the future. It could be career-related, personal, or something external like technology evolving. Write down some potential changes you might face and then brainstorm how you could prepare for or embrace those changes. By planning ahead, you'll feel more confident when the time comes.

Experiment with Small Changes

Pick one small change you can make in your daily routine this week. It could be as simple as eating lunch at a different time, trying a new workout, or spending an hour each day on a new hobby. The goal is to get comfortable with small adjustments so that bigger ones don't feel as daunting.

Mindfulness Practice

Mindfulness is a great way to stay grounded when dealing with change. Try spending 5-10 minutes each day in quiet meditation, focusing on your breath and observing your thoughts without judgment. When change happens, mindfulness helps you stay calm, clear-headed, and less reactive.

▶ Immediate Action: Create a Change Journal

To actively embrace change, start a dedicated Change Journal. This will be your personal space to reflect on, analyze, and document your experiences with change, both big and small.

Set a Regular Schedule: Choose a specific time each week to sit down with your journal—this could be Sunday evening or any time that works for you. Consistency is key.

Document Changes: Each week, write down at least two changes you've experienced. These could range from minor adjustments in your daily routine to significant life shifts.

Reflect on Your Reactions: For each change, note your initial feelings and thoughts. Did you resist? Did you embrace it? Acknowledge your emotional responses without judgment.

Identify Opportunities: After documenting your changes, ask yourself: "What potential opportunities does this change present?" Jot down any insights or possibilities that arise from the situation.

Celebrate Adaptations: Conclude each entry by celebrating your adaptability. Write down one way you adapted to the change or plan to adapt moving forward. Recognizing your ability to adjust will reinforce a positive mindset.

This journal will serve not only as a record of your experiences but also as a tool for personal growth. By consistently reflecting on change, you'll develop a deeper understanding of how to navigate future shifts with confidence and resilience.

Questions for Reflection

- Reflect on a recent change in your life that felt overwhelming. What emotions did it trigger, and how did you initially respond? How could you reframe your perspective on this change to see it as an opportunity?

- How adaptable do you consider yourself in the face of change? Are there specific situations where you find it easier or harder to embrace change? What strategies have worked for you in the past?

- When confronted with change, how often do you focus on what you can control? Can you identify moments where redirecting your focus helped you navigate change more effectively?

- Think about a time when your curiosity helped you adapt to a new situation. What questions did you ask yourself, and how did that shift your experience?

- What small changes can you implement in your daily life to strengthen your resilience to larger changes? How do you plan to incorporate these into your routine moving forward?

Conclusion: Embrace the Flow of Life

Change is an inevitable part of life, and the more we resist it, the more we struggle. But when we learn to embrace change—when we adapt, stay curious, and focus on what we can control—we become stronger, more resilient, and better prepared for whatever life throws our way.

It's not the change itself that determines whether we succeed or fail—it's how we respond to it. By developing the mindset and skills to thrive in a constantly evolving world, you're not just surviving—you're opening yourself up to new possibilities, growth, and success. So the next time change comes knocking, welcome it with open arms. You never know where it might take you.

Final Reflection

Every change, no matter how challenging, is a doorway to growth.

26

The Journey is the Reward

Life is a journey. Sounds cliché, right? You've probably heard that phrase tossed around a lot, but how often do we truly live by it? Most of us are conditioned to focus on reaching a destination, a final goal. Whether it's landing a dream job, finding the perfect relationship, or hitting a certain financial milestone, we're constantly striving to get somewhere, to achieve something. And while there's nothing wrong with having goals, here's the kicker: true wisdom and inner peace aren't found at the finish line. They're found in the journey itself.

We often think, "I'll be happy when I get there," but what if "there" never comes? Or worse, what if it comes, and it doesn't feel as fulfilling as you thought? This is why it's crucial to shift your mindset from obsessing over the end goal to appreciating the path you're on. The real magic of life happens in the present moment, not in some far-off future destination.

The Myth of Arrival

One of the biggest misconceptions we buy into is the idea that happiness is a destination. We're led to believe that if we just work hard enough, sacrifice enough, and push through enough challenges, we'll eventually reach a point where everything will be perfect. We'll be successful, content, and finally at peace.

But let's get real: there's no ultimate arrival point. There's no magical moment where life suddenly becomes easy or all your problems disappear. Even when you achieve your goals, new challenges arise. That's just how life works. So, if we're constantly waiting for some future moment to be happy, we'll be waiting forever.

Instead of getting stuck in the trap of "I'll be happy when…", ask yourself: what if happiness, wisdom, and peace are available to me right now, in this moment, regardless of whether I've reached my goals? What if the journey, with all its ups and downs, is where the real growth happens?

What if happiness, wisdom, and peace are available to me right now?

Finding Meaning in the Process

To shift your focus from the destination to the journey, you need to start finding meaning in the process. This means embracing every step of your path—the good, the bad, and the downright messy—and seeing it all as part of your personal growth.

Here's an example: think about someone training for a marathon. Yes, crossing the finish line is a big deal, but the real transformation happens in the months of preparation. The early morning runs, the sore muscles, the moments of doubt—they're all part of the journey that shapes the person into a marathon runner. It's in the process, not the result, that the person grows stronger, more resilient, and more connected to themselves.

The same goes for any area of life. Whether you're building a career, working on a relationship, or even trying to improve your health, the lessons you learn and the person you become during the journey are what truly matter.

Embrace the Present Moment

The best way to appreciate the journey is by learning to live fully in the present moment. When we're constantly focused on the future, we miss what's happening right now. We get so wrapped up in our plans and worries that we overlook the beauty and wisdom available to us in the here and now.

Think about it: how often are you really present? When you're eating, are you truly tasting your food, or are you mentally scrolling through your to-do list? When you're with friends, are you fully engaged in the conversation, or are you distracted by your phone or thinking about work?

By bringing your awareness back to the present, you start to notice the small details and moments that make life rich. The laughter of a loved one, the feel of the sun on your skin, the satisfaction of completing a task—these are the moments where life is happening. When you learn to be present, you stop waiting for some future event to make you happy. You realize that happiness is available to you right now.

Reframing Challenges as Opportunities

A big part of embracing the journey means changing how you view challenges. Often, when we encounter obstacles, we see them as roadblocks preventing us from reaching our destination. But what if, instead of being something to overcome, these challenges are actually part of the journey that's helping us grow?

Let's take the example of someone starting a business. They might face financial difficulties, rejection, and self-doubt along the way. But instead of seeing these challenges as reasons to give up, they can be viewed as opportunities to build resilience, learn new skills, and grow stronger.

Every challenge is a teacher, offering you a chance to develop qualities like patience, perseverance, and humility. If you embrace challenges instead of resisting them, you'll find that they're often the moments when you grow the most.

Wisdom in the Journey

So where does wisdom fit into all of this? Wisdom comes not from knowing all the answers or reaching a final destination, but from being open to learning as you go. When you're fully present in the journey, you start to notice the lessons that life is teaching you along the way.

Maybe you learn that you're stronger than you thought. Maybe you learn to let go of control and trust that things will work out. Or maybe you learn the importance of kindness, both to yourself and others, as you navigate difficult times.

Wisdom isn't something you achieve—it's something you cultivate through your experiences, your reflections, and your willingness to grow.

Practical Exercises to Embrace the Journey

Let's talk about how you can apply these ideas in your everyday life. Here are a few practical exercises to help you shift your focus from the destination to the journey and start finding more peace and wisdom in the present moment.

Daily Presence Practice

Set aside 5-10 minutes each day to practice being fully present. You can do this through mindfulness meditation, where you simply focus on your breath and notice the sensations in your body, or through a mindful activity like walking or eating. The goal is to bring your awareness fully into the present moment, without judgment or distraction.

As you practice this regularly, you'll find it easier to stay present throughout the day, which will help you appreciate the small moments that make up your journey.

Reframe Your Challenges

The next time you encounter a challenge, instead of viewing it as a roadblock, ask yourself: What can I learn from this? Write down at least one way this challenge is helping you grow, whether it's teaching you patience, building your resilience, or helping you develop a new skill.

This practice will help you see challenges as opportunities for growth rather than setbacks.

Celebrate Small Wins

We're often so focused on the big goals that we forget to celebrate the small victories along the way. Each day, take a moment to acknowledge the progress you've made, no matter how small. Did you finish a project? Have a good conversation with a friend? Stick to a new habit? Celebrate those moments, because they're all part of your journey.

By celebrating your small wins, you'll start to see that success isn't a destination—it's something you're already achieving every day.

Gratitude Journaling

Keep a daily gratitude journal where you write down 3-5 things you're grateful for. This helps you focus on what's going right in your life right now, rather than constantly thinking about what's missing or what's next.

Gratitude shifts your mindset from one of scarcity to one of abundance, making it easier to appreciate the journey you're on.

Set Process-Oriented Goals

Instead of only setting outcome-based goals (like losing 10 pounds or earning a certain amount of money), set goals based on the process. For example, focus on exercising 3 times a week or dedicating an hour each day to a creative project. This keeps your attention on the steps you're taking and the progress you're making, rather than obsessing over the end result.

▸ Immediate Action: Create Your Journey Map

This exercise is designed to help you visualize and appreciate the journey of your life, focusing on the lessons learned and the experiences that have shaped you.

Gather Your Materials: Grab a large piece of paper or a poster board and some colored markers or pens. If you prefer, you can also use a digital tool or app to create your map.

Draw Your Journey Line: Start by drawing a horizontal line across the middle of the page. This line represents your life journey. Mark the left end as your birth and the right end as your current age.

Identify Key Milestones: As you move along the line, identify and mark significant events in your life that have influenced who you are today. These could be achievements, challenges, relationships, or turning points. Label each milestone briefly and include the year or age when it occurred.

Reflect on Lessons Learned: Next to each milestone, write down one key lesson or insight you gained from that experience. This could be a personal strength you discovered, a skill you developed, or a realization about life.

Highlight the Present: At your current age, draw a circle and write a few words or phrases that capture how you feel about where you are right now. What are you grateful for? What do you hope to carry forward from your journey so far?

Visualize the Future: Extend the line beyond your current age, and think about the future. Write down aspirations or areas of growth you want to explore in the coming years. What experiences do you hope to add to your journey?

Review and Reflect: Take a moment to step back and look at your journey map as a whole. What patterns do you notice? How have your experiences shaped your current mindset? This visualization will help reinforce the idea that the journey itself is rich with meaning and learning.

This Journey Mapping Exercise encourages you to actively engage with your life story, appreciating the process and recognizing that every moment contributes to your growth and fulfillment.

Questions for Reflection

- What milestones in your life have significantly shaped who you are today? How did these experiences influence your beliefs and values?

- In what ways have you focused more on the destination rather than the journey? How might shifting your perspective change your current experiences?

- Can you identify any challenges in your life that turned out to be valuable learning experiences? What did you gain from them?

- How often do you take time to celebrate small victories? What small wins can you acknowledge from the past week?

- What practices can you implement in your daily life to help you stay present and appreciate the journey?

Conclusion: The Journey Is Where Life Happens

At the end of the day, life is happening right now. Not in some far-off future when you've achieved all your goals, but in the everyday moments—the challenges, the small wins, the lessons learned along the way.

When you stop focusing solely on the destination and start embracing the journey, you'll find that the wisdom and peace you've been searching for have been within you all along. It's all about being present, learning from your experiences, and enjoying the ride.

So, the next time you find yourself caught up in the future or frustrated by the challenges in front of you, remember this: the journey is the reward. Keep going, keep learning, and most importantly, keep being present. Life is happening right now, and that's where the magic is.

Final Reflection

Embrace the present and recognize that your journey is as important as any destination you seek.

27

The Road to Your Own Treasure

We all have dreams. Some are clear and vivid; others are hazy, lurking in the back of our minds, waiting for the right moment to surface. The truth is, these dreams are a part of who we are. They guide us, inspire us, and give meaning to our lives. But here's the tricky part: most of us don't chase them. We either think they're too far out of reach, or worse, we're too scared to follow the path that could lead to them.

But your dream, your own personal treasure, is worth pursuing, no matter how crazy or unrealistic it seems. The secret to finding it lies in listening to your heart. It sounds simple, right? But how often do we ignore our hearts and allow doubt, fear, or external expectations to drown out that inner voice telling us which way to go?

This chapter is all about encouraging you to listen, really listen, to what your heart is telling you and to follow your dreams with courage and determination. It's about understanding that your journey towards your treasure is the most important part of your life, even more so than the actual treasure itself. Along the way, you'll discover who you really are, what you're capable of, and what makes life truly meaningful.

Your Heart Knows the Way

There's a reason people talk about "following your heart." It's not just a cheesy phrase on a coffee mug; it's a real concept. Your heart, or your intuition, knows what will bring you joy and fulfillment, even if your mind doesn't fully understand it yet. The problem is, we tend to ignore our heart's voice. We get caught up in practicalities, like job security, societal expectations, or what other people think we should do.

But here's the thing: your heart will never steer you wrong. It's that little nudge you feel when you think about a passion you've long ignored. It's the pull you get towards something, even when it doesn't make logical sense. Listening to your heart doesn't mean being reckless or impulsive—it means tuning in to that deep, inner knowledge of what makes you feel alive and fulfilled.

Let's break it down. Have you ever had a moment where something just felt right? Maybe it was the decision to switch careers, even though it terrified you. Or maybe it was pursuing a creative project that didn't seem practical but brought you a deep sense of joy. Those moments are your heart talking.

Now, the tricky part is trusting that voice. Because often, the path your heart leads you on is full of unknowns. It's scary, uncertain, and may even seem impractical. But this is where courage comes in. You have to be brave enough to follow that pull, even if the outcome isn't guaranteed.

The Treasure is Within the Journey

As we learned before, many of us have been taught to believe that success or happiness lies in reaching a specific destination—whether it's landing your dream job, hitting a financial milestone, or finding the perfect relationship. And now we know that focusing too much on the destination can cause us to miss out on the lessons and growth that happen along the way.

You have to be brave enough to follow that pull, even if the outcome isn't guaranteed.

Yes, the treasure you're looking for isn't just at the end of the journey—it's in the journey itself. The challenges you face, the people you meet, the risks you take, and the moments of doubt and joy—they are all part of your treasure. By embracing the process, you discover more about yourself, what you're truly capable of, and what matters most to you.

For example, imagine someone who dreams of being a musician. They think that their treasure lies in becoming famous or playing in front of huge crowds. But as they work on their craft, face rejection, and continue to grow, they start to realize that the real joy is in the creation of music itself. The fame is secondary. The true treasure is the sense of fulfillment they get from expressing themselves through their art.

Overcoming Fear and Doubt

It's easy to talk about following your dreams, but the reality is, it's often terrifying. When you decide to chase something meaningful, fear and doubt are inevitable companions. What if I fail? What if I'm not good enough? What will people think? These thoughts are normal, but they shouldn't stop you.

Here's something to keep in mind: fear is a sign that you're on the right path. If you're scared, it's because what you're doing matters. Think of fear as a compass pointing you toward what's truly important. Instead of letting it paralyze you, use it as motivation to keep moving forward.

Doubt, on the other hand, often comes from comparing yourself to others or worrying about what people will say. But no one's journey is the same. Your path is unique, and your treasure is yours alone. Don't let other people's expectations or opinions dictate what you pursue.

Practical Steps to Follow Your Dreams

So, how do you actually start listening to your heart and following your dreams in a practical way? Here are some steps to help you get started:

Get Quiet and Listen. In our busy world, it's easy to get distracted by noise—both external and internal. To hear what your heart is telling you, you need to create space for stillness. Spend time alone, meditate, journal, or simply sit in silence. Ask yourself what you really want, what excites you, and what makes you feel alive. The answers are already within you, but you need to give them room to emerge.

Take Small Steps. You don't need to overhaul your entire life overnight. Start small. If your heart is pulling you towards a creative pursuit, set aside time each day to work on it. If you dream of starting your own business, begin by researching and making a plan. Small, consistent actions build momentum, and before you know it, you'll be well on your way.

Embrace Uncertainty. One of the biggest challenges in following your heart is the uncertainty that comes with it. There's no guarantee of success, but that's okay. The beauty of the journey is in the not knowing. Trust that even when the path feels unclear, you're still moving in the right direction. Be open to the unknown and understand that it's part of the process.

Learn from Setbacks. Setbacks are inevitable, but they aren't failures. They're opportunities to learn and grow. Each obstacle you encounter on your journey is a stepping stone toward your treasure. Instead of seeing setbacks as signs that you're on the wrong path, view them as necessary parts of the process. Resilience and persistence are key.

Surround Yourself with Support. It's much easier to follow your dreams when you're surrounded by people who believe in you. Seek out friends, mentors, or communities who support your vision and encourage you to keep going, even when things get tough. Positive energy is contagious, and having a supportive network can make all the difference.

Exercises to Put This Wisdom into Practice

Now that we've talked about the importance of following your heart and chasing your dreams, here are a few practical exercises to help you adopt this wisdom into your daily life.

Dream Mapping

Take a blank sheet of paper and draw a big circle in the middle. Inside the circle, write down your ultimate dream, no matter how big or small. Then, around the circle, write down all the smaller steps you can take to move closer to that dream. This exercise will help you break your big goal into manageable steps and remind you that every small action counts.

Heart Check-In

Each morning, take a few minutes to ask yourself: What is my heart telling me today? Write down whatever comes up, even if it doesn't make sense at first. This daily practice will help you tune in to your intuition and start recognizing the patterns and desires that are important to you.

Fear Journaling

Write down one thing you're afraid of when it comes to following your dream. Then, next to it, write down what you could learn or gain from facing that fear. This exercise helps reframe fear as an opportunity for growth, making it less intimidating and more manageable.

Celebrate the Journey

At the end of each day, write down one thing you're proud of or grateful for on your journey toward your dream. This could be a small action you took, a lesson you learned, or even just the fact that you kept going. Celebrating the journey will keep you motivated and focused on the progress you're making, no matter how small.

▸ Immediate Action: Create a "Heart Compass"

Take 15 minutes to create your own "Heart Compass." This is a simple visual reminder of what your heart truly desires and how it guides you toward your personal treasure. Here's how:

Materials Needed: A blank piece of paper, a pen or pencil, and colored markers or pencils (optional).

Drawing the Compass: In the center of the page, draw a small heart to represent your inner guidance. Around the heart, draw four arrows pointing outward in different directions, like a compass.

Label the Arrows: Label each arrow with something your heart is telling you to pursue. These could be dreams, passions, or things that make you feel alive. For example, the arrows could say things like "Write more," "Reconnect with nature," "Start my business," or "Prioritize family."

Reflection: Underneath your compass, write down one small action you can take for each direction. These actions don't need to be huge—they can be as simple as researching a topic, scheduling time for a creative project, or sending a message to a supportive friend.

Place it Somewhere Visible: Put your "Heart Compass" somewhere you'll see it every day, such as on your desk or by your bed. Let it remind you that your heart knows the way and that every step you take, no matter how small, is leading you toward your treasure.

This practice will help you stay connected to your dreams, and it serves as a daily motivator to take consistent action toward what truly matters to you.

Questions for Reflection

- What is one dream or passion you've been ignoring, and why? Reflect on any dreams or desires you've set aside. Are fear, doubt, or external expectations holding you back?

- When was the last time you felt deeply connected to what your heart was telling you? Consider moments in your life when you felt aligned with your true desires. What were the circumstances, and how can you create more of those moments?

- What small step can you take today to move closer to your dream? Think of one actionable thing you can do today, no matter how small, that aligns with your heart's desires.

- How do you typically respond to fear or uncertainty when following your dreams? Reflect on how you handle fear and doubt. What would change if you embraced these emotions as part of the journey rather than as roadblocks?

- What lessons have you learned from the challenges you've faced on your journey so far? Look back on obstacles you've encountered while pursuing your dreams. How have they contributed to your growth?

Conclusion: The Treasure is Yours to Find

The journey toward your personal treasure is one of the most important things you'll ever undertake. It's not always easy, and it's rarely straightforward, but it's worth every step. Your heart knows the way—you just need to listen, trust, and take action. The challenges, the setbacks, the moments of doubt—they're all part of the process that will lead you to a deeper understanding of yourself and what truly matters.

In the end, the real treasure isn't just the dream you achieve; it's the person you become along the way. So, follow your heart, embrace the journey, and trust that your treasure is waiting for you—sometimes in ways you didn't even expect.

Final Reflection

The treasure you seek is not just at the end of the path, but within each step you take. Your journey shapes you—trust it.

28

Spiritual Principles for Success and Fulfillment

When we think about success, it's easy to get caught up in material goals: a high-paying job, a big house, or achieving fame. While there's nothing wrong with wanting those things, success is about more than just external achievements. True success is about finding inner peace, fulfillment, and creating a life that aligns with your purpose. It's about feeling truly alive, connected, and content—not just with what you have, but with who you are.

To reach this kind of success, you need more than hard work and determination. You need to follow a set of principles that honor both your spiritual and personal growth. These principles are like guides that help you navigate life with more ease, joy, and clarity. The best part? They don't require you to be perfect or superhuman—they just ask that you live with intention and mindfulness.

Let's explore how they can transform the way you approach success and fulfillment.

The Power of Intention

Everything starts with intention. Whether you're setting a goal or just deciding how to approach your day, your intention shapes your reality. Think of intention as the seed you plant in the ground. Whatever you focus on with your intention, that's what you'll nurture and grow in your life.

Here's the catch: many of us set our intentions unconsciously. We let our fears, doubts, or external pressures dictate what we focus on. But when you set clear and mindful intentions, aligned with your deeper desires and values, you can direct your energy toward what truly matters.

Example: If you wake up and your first thought is, "I hope I don't mess up today," that intention is based on fear. It sets the tone for anxiety and hesitation. But if you wake up and say, "Today, I'm going to approach everything with confidence and curiosity," you're aligning yourself with positivity and growth. The difference might seem small, but it has a huge impact on how your day unfolds.

The Law of Giving and Receiving

Life operates in a flow of giving and receiving. To create harmony and success, you need to actively participate in this cycle. It's not just about giving material things—it's about sharing energy, love, support, and kindness. When you give with an open heart, you naturally invite abundance into your life.

On the flip side, receiving is just as important. Many people struggle with accepting help, compliments, or even good things that come their way. But when you block receiving, you disrupt the natural flow of energy.

Imagine you're holding a cup. If you never pour out its contents, there's no room for anything new to come in. Similarly, if you never allow yourself to receive, you block opportunities for growth and fulfillment.

Practical Application:

Give: Offer something of value to others today—your time, a compliment, a small gift, or a moment of genuine listening.

Receive: The next time someone offers you help, a compliment, or support, accept it graciously without brushing it off. Let the universe's generosity reach you.

The Principle of Detachment

One of the hardest things to master is letting go. We're often attached to outcomes, specific goals, or the way we think things should turn out. But this attachment can lead to stress, disappointment, and frustration when things don't go our way.

True success comes when you learn to detach from the outcome. That doesn't mean you stop caring or that you give up on your goals. It means you release the need to control every detail and trust that things will unfold as they're meant to.

When you let go of attachment, you open yourself to possibilities that might be even better than what you imagined.

Example: Imagine you are about to tell someone you really like, how you feel. You've been thinking about it for days, planning what you're going to say to them and hoping they feel the same way. Detachment means you allow yourself to wish they would tell you they feel the same way, but you also accept that if it doesn't happen, something or someone else - maybe even someone or something better - is on the way. You don't hold on to a specific outcome, but remain open to whatever the universe has in store for you.

The Law of Karma: Action and Reaction

Everything you do creates energy that comes back to you. This is the law of karma: every action has a consequence, good or bad. The energy you put into the world—through your thoughts, words, and actions—creates the experiences you live.

To use this principle in your favor, focus on intentional actions that align with kindness, honesty, and integrity. The more positive energy you give out, the more positive energy you'll receive in return. It's not about expecting immediate rewards, but about trusting that good actions create a ripple effect in the long run.

Example: Let's say you go out of your way to help a friend in need, even when it's inconvenient for you. That act of kindness generates positive energy. Maybe that same friend will help you down the road, or maybe a completely different opportunity will come your way because you've put kindness into the world. The universe balances itself out—what you give, you eventually get back.

Aligning with Your Purpose

Success without meaning feels empty. To experience true fulfillment, your actions need to align with your purpose—the unique contribution only you can make in this world. Discovering your purpose is not having a grand, world-changing mission. It is understanding what brings you joy, what excites you, and how you can serve others in your own way.

Start by reflecting on what makes you feel alive. Is it creating, teaching, helping others, solving problems? Whatever it is, that's a clue to your purpose. When your life aligns with your purpose, you feel energized, motivated, and successful on a deeper level.

Example: If you love solving problems, maybe your purpose is to be a guide or mentor to others who are struggling. If you find joy in creating art, your purpose might be to inspire others with your work. The key is to find what resonates with your soul and pursue it wholeheartedly.

Living in the Present Moment

We spend so much of our time either worrying about the future or dwelling on the past that we often forget to live in the present. But success and fulfillment are found here, in this moment, not in the future or past. When you're fully present, you can enjoy life's simple pleasures, make better decisions, and respond to situations with clarity.

Being present also helps you stay aligned with your deeper intentions and goals. Instead of getting lost in what might happen tomorrow or what went wrong yesterday, you can focus on what you can do right now to move closer to your dreams.

Practical Application:

Practice mindfulness by taking a few minutes each day to sit quietly and focus on your breathing. Notice the sensations in your body, the sounds around you, and how you feel in the moment. This simple practice helps train your mind to stay present.

When you find yourself worrying about the future or stuck in past regrets, gently bring your focus back to what you can control in the present.

Acceptance and Surrender

Life doesn't always go as planned. Sometimes, despite your best efforts, things fall apart. This is where acceptance comes in. Accepting what is, instead of resisting or fighting it, brings peace. Surrender doesn't mean giving up—it means trusting the process and understanding that everything happens for a reason, even if that reason isn't immediately clear.

When you practice acceptance, you allow yourself to flow with life instead of against it. You become more resilient, flexible, and open to new opportunities that might arise from unexpected challenges.

> *Accepting what is, instead of resisting or fighting it, brings peace.*

Example: If you experience a setback—a job loss, a failed relationship, or a personal challenge—accept it without resistance. Instead of asking, "Why did this happen to me?" shift your mindset to, "What can I learn from this?" Surrendering to the experience allows you to grow and move forward with grace.

Practical Exercises to Apply These Principles

Now that we've explored these spiritual principles, let's get practical. Here are some exercises to help you start living these principles every day.

Set a Daily Intention

Each morning, before you start your day, set a clear and mindful intention. This could be something like, "Today, I will approach everything with a positive mindset" or "I will be kind and generous in my interactions." Write it down and revisit it throughout the day to keep yourself aligned with your purpose.

Practice Gratitude

Take a few minutes each evening to write down three things you're grateful for. This simple exercise helps you stay present, appreciate what you have, and create positive energy that will attract more good things into your life.

Acts of Kindness

Make it a habit to give something each day—whether it's your time, attention, or support. By contributing positively to the world around you, you engage in the law of giving and receiving.

Let Go of Control

Identify one area of your life where you're holding on too tightly—whether it's a relationship, a career goal, or a personal expectation. Practice letting go of the need to control the outcome. Trust that whatever happens is for your growth and highest good.

Live in the Moment

Throughout the day, remind yourself to pause and check in with the present. When you're eating, focus on the flavors. When you're with a friend, give them your full attention. These small moments of mindfulness help train your mind to stay present and enjoy the journey.

▶ Immediate Action: A Day of Conscious Giving and Receiving

Commit to spending your entire day actively engaging in both giving and receiving, with mindfulness and awareness. Start by giving something of value—whether it's a compliment, a small act of service, or even your time and attention to someone in need. Notice the energy you put out into the world, and how it feels to give without expecting anything in return.

Later in the day, focus on receiving. Pay attention to the compliments, help, or kindness that others extend to you. Instead of deflecting or brushing it off, fully accept it with gratitude and grace. Reflect on how allowing yourself to receive opens you up to the natural flow of abundance.

At the end of the day, journal about how this conscious practice impacted your sense of balance, connection, and fulfillment. How did giving and receiving affect your energy and outlook?

Questions for Reflection

- What intentions am I setting daily, and are they aligned with my deeper values and purpose? How can I shift my intentions to reflect what truly matters to me, rather than reacting to external pressures or fears?

- In what ways do I struggle with giving or receiving? Do I find it easier to give but harder to accept help or kindness, or vice versa? How can I create more balance in the flow of giving and receiving in my life?

- What attachments am I holding onto that cause me stress or disappointment? How would my experience of life change if I practiced detachment and trusted in the process more?

- How have my past actions, whether intentional or unconscious, shaped my present reality? What small actions can I start taking today to align with the positive energy I want to experience in the future?

- Am I truly living in the present moment, or do I spend too much time worrying about the future or dwelling on the past? What steps can I take to bring more mindfulness and presence into my daily life?

Conclusion: Success Beyond the Material

By following these spiritual principles, you'll find that success becomes less related to what you have and more related to who you are. You'll experience a deeper sense of fulfillment, peace, and purpose, no matter where you are on your journey. Success isn't just about reaching a destination—it's about how you live every day, with intention, kindness, and trust.

The path to success is a spiritual one. So, as you move forward, keep these principles in mind, and watch how your life begins to align with your highest potential. Your journey has just begun.

Final Reflection

Everything you seek is already within you.

29

The Healing Power of Your Mind

Imagine waking up one morning and realizing that you hold within yourself an untapped power to heal your body. No, it's not magic, and it's not some impossible fantasy. This power is rooted in something you use every day: your mind. Yes, your thoughts, beliefs, and intentions have the potential to influence your body in profound ways.

You've likely heard stories of people who experienced miraculous recoveries from serious illnesses, and maybe you chalked it up to luck, fate, or divine intervention. But what if the real magic behind those recoveries was something far more accessible—something you could tap into right now? The truth is, your mind can play a significant role in your body's healing process. When you align your beliefs and intentions with a deep sense of conviction, your body responds.

In this chapter, we'll explore how the mind can heal the body, and more importantly, how you can harness this incredible ability in your own life. By the end, you'll have practical tools to start using the power of your mind to enhance your well-being.

The Science of Belief: How Your Mind Affects Your Body

Let's start with some basics. Your thoughts and beliefs don't just float around in your head—they trigger physical responses in your body. When you think a happy thought, your body releases feel-good chemicals like dopamine and serotonin. When you're stressed or anxious, your body floods with cortisol, a stress hormone. This is called the mind-body connection, and it's not just a theory; it's a scientifically supported fact.

The most well-known example of the mind influencing the body is the placebo effect. You've probably heard about this: patients given sugar pills or harmless saline injections sometimes get better, not because of the pill or the injection, but because they believe they're receiving a real treatment. Their mind believes it's healing, and the body follows.

> *When you align your beliefs and intentions with a deep sense of conviction, your body responds.*

What's fascinating is that this effect can be so powerful that it often produces measurable, real changes in the body—like lowering blood pressure or reducing pain. If belief alone can trigger these outcomes, imagine what might happen if you consciously harnessed the power of your mind to create change in your body.

The Role of Intention: Directing Your Healing Power

Belief is one part of the equation, but it's intention that directs that belief like a laser beam. When you set an intention, you're sending a clear message to your body about what you want to happen. This isn't wishful thinking; it's focusing your mental energy in a way that your body can understand.

Think of intention as a form of communication with your cells. When you intend to heal, you're giving your body a signal: "It's time to get to work." Your cells start responding by making the necessary biochemical changes to support your intention. Your brain has the ability to rewire itself based on your thoughts, beliefs, and experiences.

For example, athletes often use visualization to mentally rehearse their performance before stepping onto the field. They imagine themselves succeeding—scoring a goal, making a perfect dive, or crossing the finish line first. This mental rehearsal activates the same brain circuits as actually doing the activity, which helps improve their real-world performance. Similarly, when you set an intention for healing, you activate pathways in your brain that help your body move toward that outcome.

How Belief and Intention Shape Your Reality

Belief and intention go hand in hand. Think of belief as the fuel and intention as the engine. Together, they can drive real change in your body. But here's the catch: it has to be genuine. Half-hearted belief or vague intentions aren't going to cut it. Your mind and body know when you're just going through the motions. To create real change, you have to fully believe that your body is capable of healing and set a clear intention for what you want that healing to look like.

This doesn't mean ignoring medical advice or thinking you can heal every ailment with thoughts alone. It does mean acknowledging that your mindset plays a crucial role in the healing process. By believing in your body's capacity to heal and aligning your intentions with that belief, you're setting the stage for remarkable outcomes.

Practical Steps to Harness the Healing Power of Your Mind

So here are some steps you can take to start using your mind's power to heal your body.

Change the Story You Tell Yourself

What do you believe about your body? Do you see yourself as someone who gets sick easily or has a hard time recovering from illness? If so, it's time to rewrite that story.

Exercise: Start by paying attention to the way you talk about your health. Do you often say things like, "I always get colds in the winter," or "I have terrible genetics"? These beliefs become self-fulfilling prophecies. Instead, start affirming that your body is strong and resilient. Use phrases like, "My body knows how to heal itself," or "I trust my body's ability to recover." Write these affirmations down and repeat them daily until they become part of your internal narrative.

Visualize Your Healing

One of the most powerful tools you can use is visualization. Just like athletes use visualization to improve their performance, you can use it to improve your health.

Exercise: Set aside 10 minutes each day to sit quietly and visualize your body healing. Picture your cells repairing themselves, your immune system strengthening, and any illness or pain dissolving. Imagine how good it feels to be healthy and vibrant. This isn't just daydreaming; it's about creating a mental blueprint for your body to follow.

Meditation and Mindfulness

Meditation is an excellent way to quiet your mind and focus your intentions. When you meditate, you train your brain to stay present and avoid getting caught up in fear or negative thinking, which can be detrimental to the healing process.

Exercise: Start with a simple mindfulness meditation. Find a quiet place to sit, close your eyes, and focus on your breath. As thoughts arise, acknowledge them without judgment and return your focus to your breathing. You don't need to meditate for hours—a few minutes each day can make a significant difference in reducing stress and promoting healing.

Set Clear Healing Intentions

As we discussed earlier, intention is key. To tap into the healing power of your mind, you need to set clear, specific intentions for your health.

Exercise: Each morning, before you start your day, set an intention for your body. It could be something like, "Today, I intend to nourish my body and allow it to heal," or "I release any tension and allow my body to be at peace." These intentions don't have to be complicated, but they should be positive and focused on what you want to achieve.

Release Limiting Beliefs

Limiting beliefs are those pesky thoughts that hold you back—like, "I can't heal because my illness is too advanced," or "It's too late for me to feel better." These beliefs can become mental roadblocks to your healing.

Exercise: Write down a list of any limiting beliefs you have about your health. Then, challenge each one. Ask yourself, "Is this belief absolutely true?" You'll often find that many of these beliefs are based on fear rather than fact. Once you've identified your limiting beliefs, replace them with empowering ones, like "My body is capable of healing in ways I haven't yet imagined."

Surround Yourself with Positivity

The people and environments you surround yourself with can either support your healing or detract from it. Negative energy and toxic relationships can weaken your mental and physical well-being, while positive, uplifting environments can boost your mood and help your body heal.

Exercise: Take inventory of your surroundings. Are there people or situations that drain your energy? If so, try to minimize your exposure to them. Instead, seek out positive influences—spend time with people who support and uplift you, and create a home environment that feels peaceful and nurturing.

▶ Immediate Action: Cultivate Healing by Aligning Mind and Body

Your body has an innate ability to heal itself, but harnessing the power of your mind can amplify this process. In this exercise, you'll learn to shift your mindset, focus your intention, and create an environment that supports your body's natural healing abilities.

1. Identify a Healing Need:

Begin by identifying one area of your body or health where you desire healing or improvement. Whether it's physical pain, illness, or even emotional stress, take a moment to clearly define this area of focus. Write down what you're currently experiencing, describing both physical sensations and emotional reactions related to it.

2. Shift Your Narrative:

Next, recognize the story you've been telling yourself about this area of your health. For example, if you've been saying, "This pain always gets worse," or "I never seem to heal," it's time to reframe that narrative. Write a new story that emphasizes your body's strength and potential for healing. For instance, say, "My body is capable of healing itself," or "Every day, I am getting stronger and healthier." By rewriting this story, you set the foundation for healing by shifting from a negative mindset to one of possibility and growth.

3. Create a Healing Visualization:

Now, close your eyes and visualize your body healing. Picture the specific area where you need healing—whether it's an aching joint, an organ, or a general sense of wellness—and imagine your cells working in harmony to restore balance and vitality. See your body as vibrant, whole, and healthy. Imagine any discomfort melting away and being replaced by a sense of peace and strength. Feel the warmth of healing energy spreading through that part of your body, and hold this image for several minutes.

4. Set a Healing Intention:

Set a clear intention for your body's healing. This could be a simple affirmation such as, "Today, I choose to nourish my body and allow it to heal," or "I trust in my body's wisdom to restore balance and health." Write down this intention and keep it somewhere visible, revisiting it throughout the day to remind yourself that your mind and body are working together in harmony.

5. Release Limiting Beliefs About Healing:

Write down any limiting beliefs you hold about your body's ability to heal. These might include thoughts like, "This is just how my body is," or "I'll never fully recover." Now, challenge these beliefs. Ask yourself, "Is this belief absolutely true?" For each limiting belief, write a positive, empowering belief to replace it. For example, replace "I never heal quickly" with "My body heals at the perfect pace for me." This process helps clear mental barriers that may be preventing your body from achieving its full healing potential.

6. Take Action for Physical Support:

Healing isn't just a mental process—your body also needs physical support. Take one actionable step to support your body's health. This could be drinking more water, eating a nourishing meal, stretching, or getting sufficient rest. By combining intentional action with mental practices, you reinforce your body's healing process holistically.

By consistently focusing on the positive potential within you, you create a powerful environment where your mind and body can thrive together.

Questions for Reflection

- How do your current beliefs about your body and health shape your approach to healing? Are they empowering or limiting?

- Can you recall a time when your mindset positively or negatively impacted your physical health or recovery? What lessons can you draw from that experience?

- What role does intention play in your daily life, particularly regarding your well-being? Are you consciously setting intentions for your health and healing?

- In what ways can you incorporate more positive, healing-focused thoughts into your routine? How might this change your relationship with your body?

- Are there any limiting beliefs you hold about your body's ability to heal? How can you begin to challenge and reframe them to foster a more supportive mindset?

- How do you feel when you focus on the idea of your body being capable of healing itself? What emotions or resistances come up, and how can you work through them?

Conclusion: You Are the Placebo

The idea that your mind has the power to heal your body is both empowering and transformative. By shifting your beliefs, setting clear intentions, and aligning your thoughts with a positive, healing mindset, you can create real, measurable change in your physical well-being. This doesn't mean you should ignore medical treatments or rely solely on your mind for healing, but it does mean that your mindset can be a powerful ally in your journey to better health.

So, as you move forward, remember: you are the placebo. Your beliefs, thoughts, and intentions hold the power to shape your reality. Start harnessing that power today, and watch how your body responds to the message of healing you send it.

Final Reflection

The power to heal resides within you, shaped by your beliefs, intentions, and willingness to embrace your body's innate wisdom.

30

The Transformative Power of Your Mind and Positive Affirmations

What if the things you say to yourself, whether consciously or not, are guiding the entire course of your life?

Sounds powerful, right? Well, the truth is, this is exactly what's happening. Our minds hold incredible power to shape our experiences, and one of the most effective ways to tap into that power is through positive affirmations. These are simple, yet powerful statements that, when repeated with intention, shift your mindset, boost your confidence, and as we just have learned, even help heal your body.

In this chapter, we'll see how positive affirmations influence your reality and how to reprogram limiting beliefs to create a life that feels good inside and out.

Your Mind: The Architect of Your Life

Your mind is like a constant storyteller, narrating your experiences, shaping your responses, and influencing your future. The thoughts you think every day are constructing the world you live in. If you're constantly telling yourself things like "I never have any luck," or "This always happens to me", your life is going to reflect that narrative.

The good news? Just as negative thoughts can keep you stuck, positive ones can help you break free. The mind doesn't care whether the thoughts it's repeating are true or not. It simply acts on the patterns it's given. So, if you can change the script running in your head, you can begin to shift your reality in profound ways.

It's like having a direct line to the universe. The things you focus on, grow. If you're always thinking about lack, fear, or failure, you're likely to attract more of that. But if you train your mind to focus on abundance, love, and success, suddenly, doors start to open where there were only walls before.

The things you focus on, grow.

The Power of Positive Affirmations

So, how do you change the script? That's where positive affirmations come in.

An affirmation is a positive statement you repeat to yourself regularly to rewire your thought patterns. It might sound like this: "I am worthy of love and respect," or "I am capable of achieving my goals." At first glance, this might seem too simple to actually work, but here's the magic: repeated affirmations start to overwrite the old, negative scripts running in your subconscious mind. The more you say them, the more your mind begins to believe them—and the more your life begins to reflect these new beliefs.

Think of affirmations as mental training. Just like lifting weights strengthens your muscles, repeating positive affirmations strengthens your mind. Over time, they become second nature, transforming the way you see yourself and the world.

The Science Behind It

If you're wondering whether this is just wishful thinking, there's actual science backing it up. As we learned in the previous chapter, our brains are constantly forming new connections—a phenomenon known as neuroplasticity. So the way we think can literally change the structure of our brains. When you repeat positive affirmations, you're creating new neural pathways. Over time, those pathways become stronger and more dominant, making it easier for you to think positively by default.

It's like rerouting a river. At first, it's going to take some effort to get the water flowing in a new direction. But once you've established a new path, the water (or in this case, your thoughts) will naturally follow that route.

How to Craft Effective Affirmations

Not all affirmations are created equal. To create affirmations that will genuinely impact your life, there are a few guidelines to follow:

- **Keep them in the present tense**. Affirmations should be phrased as if what you want is already happening. For example, instead of saying, "I will be happy," say, "I am happy." This helps trick your brain into believing it's true right now.

- **Make them specific and positive**. Focus on what you want, not what you're trying to avoid. For instance, instead of saying, "I don't want to be stressed," try, "I am calm and in control."

- **Believe in them**. The more conviction you have when saying your affirmations, the faster they'll take root. If it feels awkward at first, that's okay. With time, your belief in these statements will grow.

- **Repeat, repeat, repeat**. Affirmations work through repetition. The more often you say them—whether aloud, in your head, or written down—the stronger their impact will be.

Putting Affirmations to Work: A Day in the Life

Let's imagine a typical day where you consciously use affirmations to transform your experience.

Morning: You wake up, and instead of checking your phone immediately, you take a moment to center yourself. You say out loud: "Today, I choose peace and positivity. Everything I need comes to me effortlessly." Already, you've set the tone for your day.

During your commute: Maybe you're stuck in traffic or riding a crowded bus. Instead of letting frustration take over, you silently repeat an affirmation: "I am calm, patient, and in control of my reactions." You notice your tension easing as you focus on these words.

At work: Perhaps you're facing a challenging project, and self-doubt starts creeping in. Rather than spiraling into negative thinking, you pause and affirm: "I am capable, focused, and creative. I find solutions easily." This shift in mindset helps you tackle the problem with renewed energy.

Before bed: At the end of the day, you take a few minutes to reflect and say: "I am grateful for the abundance in my life. I am at peace." This helps you wind down and puts you in a positive, restful state before sleep.

Overcoming Resistance: Why You Might Feel Silly at First

Here's the deal: you might feel a little awkward or even ridiculous when you start using affirmations. That's totally normal! Most of us are so used to talking negatively to ourselves that positive statements feel foreign. But like any new habit, the more you practice, the easier it becomes.

Remember, your subconscious mind is always listening. If you've spent years telling yourself that you're not good enough, it might take some time to reverse that pattern. But with persistence, you'll start to notice shifts in how you feel and how you approach challenges.

Exercises to Embrace the Power of Affirmations

Now that you understand the power of your mind and how affirmations work, it's time to put this wisdom into practice. These exercises will help you harness the transformative power of your thoughts and start creating the life you truly want.

Create Your Personal Affirmation List

Start by identifying areas of your life where you want to see improvement. Whether it's self-confidence, career success, health, or relationships, craft affirmations tailored to those areas.

Exercise: Write down 5-10 positive affirmations that resonate with you. Here are a few examples to inspire you:

- "I am worthy of love and respect."
- "Opportunities flow to me easily and effortlessly."
- "My body is healthy, strong, and capable of healing."
- "I trust myself and my ability to make the right decisions."
- "I attract positivity and joy into my life."

Read these affirmations out loud every morning and before bed. Notice how they start to influence your mindset over time.

Affirmation Journaling

Journaling is a powerful way to amplify the effects of your affirmations. Writing things down creates a deeper connection between your conscious mind and your intentions.

Exercise: Each day, write down your top three affirmations in a journal. As you write, take a moment to truly feel the words. Visualize what your life looks like when these affirmations are your reality. You can also reflect on any shifts you notice in your thoughts or behaviors as you consistently use these affirmations.

Mirror Work

Looking into your own eyes while speaking affirmations adds an extra layer of intensity and conviction.

Exercise: Stand in front of a mirror, look yourself in the eyes, and say your affirmations out loud. It might feel uncomfortable at first, but this practice can help you develop a deeper sense of self-love and belief in your affirmations. Do this for a few minutes each day, and notice how your confidence and sense of self-worth start to grow.

▶ Immediate Action: Affirmation Integration for Daily Empowerment

Positive affirmations can shift your mindset and help you align with your desired reality. This exercise is designed to help you integrate affirmations into your daily life in a meaningful, empowering way, enhancing the impact of each affirmation.

Morning Affirmation Ritual

Start your day by choosing a single affirmation that resonates with your current goals or emotional state. Before getting out of bed, sit for a moment, take a deep breath, and say your chosen affirmation out loud. For example, "I am confident, capable, and worthy of success." Repeat it three times, slowly and with intention, allowing the words to fully sink in. Visualize how this affirmation will guide your actions throughout the day.

Set Reminders Throughout Your Day

Program your phone or write a reminder in a visible place (e.g., a sticky note on your mirror or desk) to prompt you to repeat your affirmation during key moments in your day—like before an important meeting, conversation, or decision. This keeps the affirmation active in your mind, helping you stay grounded and focused on your intention.

Evening Reflection and Affirmation Adjustment

At the end of the day, take a few minutes to reflect on how the affirmation influenced your thoughts, feelings, and actions. Did you notice any shifts in your mindset or behavior? If you found the affirmation helpful, carry it into the next day. If not, adjust it to better fit your needs for tomorrow. The key is to stay flexible and responsive to what resonates most with your current journey.

Affirmation Journaling

In addition to your ritual, maintain a journal dedicated to your affirmations. Each night, write down the day's affirmation and any noticeable changes in your outlook or behavior. Use this space to reflect on how these positive statements are gradually shaping your mindset and contributing to your overall well-being.

This ritual weaves affirmations into the fabric of your daily routine, reinforcing their impact on your mindset and emotional state. By consistently integrating these powerful statements, you empower yourself to create lasting, positive change.

Questions for Reflection

- How do you currently speak to yourself, both in moments of success and in times of challenge? Are your internal dialogues more positive or negative?

- Can you identify a specific belief about yourself that may be holding you back? How could you reframe that belief into an empowering affirmation?

- Think about a time when you used positive thinking or affirmations—what impact did it have on your mindset, actions, or outcomes? How could consistent practice deepen that impact?

- How do you feel when you repeat affirmations? Do you notice resistance, discomfort, or ease? What might these feelings reveal about your current beliefs?

- In what areas of your life could you most benefit from reprogramming negative thought patterns through affirmations?

- How might your life change if you consistently replaced self-doubt with affirmations of confidence, worthiness, and capability?

- How does the concept of neuroplasticity empower you to take control of your mindset and reshape your life?

Conclusion: The Life You Desire Is Within Reach

Your mind is your most powerful tool, and affirmations are the key to unlocking its potential. As you begin this journey, remember that real change takes time. Be patient with yourself, stay committed, and trust the process. Before long, you'll notice the incredible shifts happening in your mindset, your health, and your life as a whole.

Your thoughts create your reality—so why not choose thoughts that create the reality you want?

Final Reflection

What you cultivate in your mind will grow into the life you experience.

31

The Joy in Everyday Moments

When was the last time you stopped to savor a cup of coffee, really noticing the warmth of the mug in your hands, the aroma rising up to greet your senses, and the first sip that floods your mouth with flavor? Or when did you last take a walk and let yourself be fully present, feeling the sun on your skin or the breeze play with your hair, instead of rushing through your to-do list in your head?

These small, seemingly ordinary moments are the very threads that can weave joy into the fabric of our daily lives. Too often, we overlook them, thinking that happiness only comes in big, monumental doses—like landing a dream job, going on a vacation, or celebrating a major milestone. But the truth is, joy lives in the everyday moments, the ones we often miss because we're too busy waiting for something grander to come along.

Finding joy in the small things means cultivating a mindset that allows you to see the beauty, peace, and happiness that already exist in the present. It's rewiring your brain to appreciate what's right in front of you, no matter how simple or routine it might seem. In this chapter, we'll explore how you can start seeing the world through this lens of everyday joy and how doing so can make a profound difference in your overall well-being.

Why Small Moments Matter

Imagine you're building a house. The grand structure isn't made out of one giant piece of material—it's built brick by brick. The same goes for your happiness. It's not created by one single, life-changing event, but by a series of small, joyful moments that accumulate over time. Each little moment is a brick that adds to the overall structure of your well-being.

The problem is, many of us get stuck in a mindset of waiting for happiness. We tell ourselves, "I'll be happy when...": when I get that promotion, when I move to a new city, when I finally have time for a proper vacation. But this mindset keeps pushing happiness just out of reach, always tied to some future event. In the meantime, we're missing out on the joy that's already available to us in our everyday lives.

Shifting your focus to the small moments is realizing that you can find fulfillment and happiness right here, right now, in the life you're already living. And when you do, you'll notice that the bigger, more exciting moments become even more meaningful because you've trained yourself to live fully in the present.

The Science of Everyday Joy

There's actually some fascinating science behind this idea. Our brains are wired to prioritize the big, dramatic experiences because, evolutionarily speaking, these were the moments that kept us safe or pushed us to survive. But that doesn't mean we're stuck with that wiring forever. The human brain has something called neuroplasticity, which means it can change and adapt. You can train your brain to focus more on positive experiences, no matter how small they may seem.

When you start paying attention to the little things that bring you joy, your brain begins to strengthen the neural pathways that support positive thinking and emotional resilience. This means you'll start to experience more joy simply because you've taught your brain to look for it.

Think of it like this: Your brain is a camera, and whatever you point it at is what you'll notice most. If you're constantly focused on stress, problems, and what's missing from your life, that's what will dominate your mental space. But if you start pointing your mental camera toward the small moments of joy—whether it's a good conversation with a friend, the feeling of accomplishment after completing a task, or even just noticing the colors of the sunset—your brain will start picking up on more of those moments naturally.

Practical Ways to Find Joy in the Everyday

So, how do you start finding more joy in your daily life? It's actually simpler than you might think. The key is mindfulness and intentionality—making a conscious effort to slow down and appreciate the present moment. Here are some practical tips to help you start embracing the joy in the small things.

> *You'll start to experience more joy simply because you've taught your brain to look for it.*

Start with Gratitude

One of the easiest ways to find joy in your day-to-day life is to practice gratitude. When you actively look for things to be grateful for, your brain starts scanning your environment for positive experiences. Something as small as enjoying a hot shower or having a productive morning can be enough.

Exercise: At the end of each day, write down three things you're grateful for. Try to focus on small, specific moments that brought you joy, like "I'm grateful for the way the sunlight streamed through my window during breakfast," or "I'm thankful for the five minutes of quiet I had to enjoy my tea." Over time, this practice will train your brain to notice these joyful moments more often.

Create Small Rituals

Daily rituals can help anchor you in the present moment, giving you something to look forward to and enjoy. These don't have to be elaborate—think of them as little acts of self-care that you intentionally weave into your day.

Exercise: Create a morning or evening ritual that's just for you. It could be something like spending five minutes stretching, sitting with your coffee before diving into your day, or listening to your favorite song on your commute. The key is to make this time about enjoying the moment, rather than rushing through it.

Savor Simple Pleasures

We tend to rush through life, often too focused on the next task to enjoy what's happening right now. But by slowing down and fully engaging with even the simplest of activities, you can turn the ordinary into something extraordinary.

Exercise: The next time you're doing something mundane—washing dishes, taking a walk, or even folding laundry—pause and focus on the sensory details. What does the water feel like on your hands? What sounds can you hear as you walk? When you focus on these details, you can turn even the most routine activities into moments of mindfulness and joy.

Be Present in Your Interactions

A lot of joy comes from connection with others, but we often miss out on it because we're not fully present. The next time you're with someone—whether it's a friend, family member, or even a co-worker—try to be completely engaged in the conversation. Listen without distractions and appreciate the moment for what it is.

Exercise: Challenge yourself to have a distraction-free conversation at least once a day. Put your phone away, turn off the TV, and really focus on the person in front of you. Notice how it feels to give and receive attention without interruptions, and see how this deepens your connection.

Celebrate Small Wins

Big achievements don't come around every day, but small wins happen all the time—and they're worth celebrating! Whether you've finished a project, cooked a meal you're proud of, or simply made it through a tough day, take a moment to acknowledge your effort and success.

Exercise: At the end of each week, write down your "small wins." These can be anything from "I made it to the gym twice" to "I had a great conversation with a friend." Celebrating these small victories helps reinforce a sense of progress and joy in your everyday life.

Finding Joy When Times Are Tough

Of course, life isn't always sunshine and rainbows. There will be hard days, difficult seasons, and moments when joy feels far away. But even during challenging times, you can still find small pockets of joy if you look for them. In fact, this practice becomes even more important during tough times because it helps you maintain resilience and hope.

During these times, don't force yourself to be happy all the time—honor your emotions. But also remind yourself that joy and sorrow can coexist. You can have a tough day and still find joy in a warm hug, a comforting meal, or a few minutes of quiet. These moments may seem small, but they carry great weight when you need them most.

Exercises for Cultivating Joy in Your Daily Life

Here are a few additional exercises to help you embrace the joy in everyday moments and make this practice a natural part of your life.

Joy Jar

Find a jar or box, and each day, write down one thing that brought you joy on a small piece of paper. It could be something as simple as "the smell of fresh bread" or "a compliment from a colleague." Over time, you'll create a visual reminder of all the joyful moments in your life. On tough days, you can pull out a few notes and remind yourself of the happiness that exists, even in hard times.

Mindful Morning Moments

Start your day by taking five minutes to notice the joy around you. This could be while you're making breakfast, brushing your teeth, or even just sitting quietly. Pay attention to your senses—what you see, hear, feel, and smell—and notice the little things that bring you joy, like the warmth of your coffee cup or the first light of day.

Gratitude Walk

Take a short walk each day, either around your neighborhood or somewhere you enjoy. As you walk, focus on noticing things you're grateful for. It could be the way the trees sway in the wind, the sound of birds, or even the feeling of the ground beneath your feet. This simple practice can help you feel more connected to the present and increase your awareness of the small joys all around you.

▶ Immediate Action: Joy Snapshot Challenge

Set a timer on your phone or choose a time during your day when you'll pause for one minute. During this minute, take a "snapshot" of a joyful moment around you, mentally or literally with your camera. It could be anything—a flower blooming, a child's laughter, a sip of your favorite drink, or even the feeling of sunlight on your skin.

Once you capture that moment, take a deep breath and immerse yourself fully in it. Reflect on what makes this moment special and how it connects you to the present. Jot down a brief description of your experience in a notebook or your phone at the end of the day. By regularly capturing these small moments of joy, you'll train your mind to notice the beauty already surrounding you.

Do this for one week and notice how your awareness of joyful moments grows.

Questions for Reflection

- How often do I pause to appreciate the small moments of joy in my daily life? What keeps me from doing so more often?
- Can I recall a recent simple moment that brought me unexpected joy? How did it make me feel, and why did I notice it?

- In what ways could I bring more intentionality to my day-to-day routine to experience more joy in ordinary moments?

- How does my current mindset about happiness affect my ability to appreciate joy in the present? Am I constantly waiting for "big" moments to feel happy?

- What small daily rituals can I create to invite more mindfulness and presence into my life?

Conclusion: Embrace the Beauty of the Everyday

Joy doesn't have to be something you wait for or chase after. It's already here, in the small, often overlooked moments of your everyday life. By shifting your focus and training your mind to see these moments, you can cultivate a deeper sense of happiness, contentment, and peace.

The grand moments in life are wonderful, but it's the accumulation of small joys that makes for a truly rich and fulfilling life. So, start today. Slow down, pay attention, and let the simple pleasures of life bring a smile to your face.

The joy you're seeking is already within reach—you just need to notice it.

Final Reflection

True joy doesn't wait for extraordinary circumstances; it lives quietly in the ordinary. The more you train your mind to notice it, the more it reveals itself.

32

The Journey Within – Discovering Yourself to Find Freedom

Imagine carrying an invisible armor around with you every single day. It's there to protect you from the world—to guard you against pain, rejection, and failure. At first, it feels like a shield, something that keeps you safe. But over time, that armor becomes heavy. It starts to rust. And the longer you carry it, the more it weighs you down. Eventually, you forget how to take it off. This "armor" represents the walls we build around ourselves—the beliefs, fears, and defenses that keep us from truly knowing who we are.

This chapter is about breaking free from that invisible armor and realizing that true freedom, peace, and happiness don't come from external success or approval but from within. The process of self-exploration and self-knowledge is the key to unlocking that freedom.

Why Self-Exploration and Self-Knowledge Matter

The world we live in often teaches us to look outward for answers. We're taught to chase achievements, to compare ourselves to others, and to measure our worth by external standards. But when we do that, we lose touch with the most important person in our lives: ourselves.

Think about it—how well do you truly know yourself? What are your deepest fears, desires, and dreams? What beliefs are you carrying that may not even be your own but were handed down to you by society, your family, or past experiences? Without exploring these questions, you risk living a life that's not fully yours—a life based on expectations rather than authentic fulfillment.

Self-exploration is the process of peeling back the layers of conditioning, defense mechanisms, and false beliefs that have built up over time. It's understanding your true essence—the person you are when you strip away the roles you play and the masks you wear.

Self-knowledge, on the other hand, is the wisdom that comes from this exploration. It's the clarity and understanding of who you are at your core. And when you have that clarity, you can make choices that align with your true self rather than choices based on fear or societal pressure. You become free—not just free from others' expectations, but free from the limitations you've placed on yourself.

> *True freedom, peace, and happiness don't come from external success or approval but from within.*

Breaking Free from Your "Armor"

Our inner "armor" starts to form early in life. We build it piece by piece as a way to protect ourselves from getting hurt. Maybe you were told as a child to always be strong, never cry, or to hide your true feelings to avoid being judged. Over time, these protective behaviors harden into beliefs like "I must always be perfect," or "I can't show vulnerability because it's a sign of weakness."

But here's the thing: while that armor might keep you from feeling pain, it also prevents you from experiencing joy, love, and true connection. It keeps you trapped in a state of constant defense, never allowing yourself to fully live.

To truly find freedom, you have to begin the journey of self-exploration. This means looking inward and being willing to face parts of yourself that you've buried or ignored. It can be uncomfortable at first—like stepping into the unknown—but it's the only way to shed the armor and reconnect with your authentic self.

Steps for Self-Exploration and Self-Knowledge

Let's dive into some practical steps that will help you begin this journey. Remember, self-exploration isn't something you do once and then check off your list—it's an ongoing process that deepens over time. The more you practice it, the more clarity and freedom you'll find.

Start by Observing Your Thoughts and Emotions

Before you can change anything, you first need to understand it. That's why the first step to self-exploration is simply observing your thoughts and emotions without judgment. Pay attention to the patterns that come up in your mind—especially the negative or limiting ones. What do you tell yourself when things go wrong? Do you blame yourself or others? Do you avoid difficult emotions or try to numb them?

Exercise: Set aside 10 minutes each day to sit quietly and observe your thoughts. You don't need to do anything with them—just notice what comes up. If you feel judgment creeping in (for example, if you catch yourself thinking "I shouldn't be feeling this way"), gently acknowledge it and let it go. This practice will help you become more aware of your inner dialogue, which is the first step toward understanding yourself better.

Question Your Beliefs

We all carry beliefs about ourselves and the world, but many of these beliefs aren't necessarily true—they're just stories we've been telling ourselves for years. For example, you might believe "I'm not strong enough," or "I don't deserve happiness," but where did those beliefs come from? Are they really true, or are they based on past experiences or what someone else told you?

Exercise: Write down one limiting belief you have about yourself.

It could be something like "I'm not smart enough" or "I'll never find love." Once you've identified it, ask yourself:

- Where did this belief come from?
- Is it based on facts or assumptions?
- How has this belief been holding me back?
- What would my life look like if I didn't believe this anymore?

Challenging your beliefs is a powerful way to start breaking down the mental armor that's keeping you stuck.

Connect with Your Authentic Self

Who are you when no one's watching? What do you love doing simply because it makes you feel alive, not because it impresses others or meets some external standard? These are questions that help you reconnect with your authentic self—the part of you that's been buried beneath the roles, expectations, and responsibilities.

Exercise: Think back to when you were a child. What did you love doing before anyone told you what you "should" do? Was it painting, playing outside, reading, or daydreaming? Spend some time reconnecting with these activities and see how they make you feel. This isn't about being productive or achieving anything but experiencing joy and freedom through your natural interests and passions.

Embrace Vulnerability

One of the hardest parts of self-exploration is being vulnerable—not just with others, but with yourself. It's easier to stay guarded, to avoid the messy and uncomfortable parts of who we are. But by now I'm sure you already know that vulnerability is where growth occurs. It's where we discover our true strength and resilience.

Being vulnerable means being honest with yourself and others. It's acknowledging that you don't have all the answers and that it's okay to ask for help or admit when you're struggling. The more you embrace vulnerability, the more authentic and free you'll feel.

Exercise: The next time you catch yourself trying to put on a "mask" (whether it's pretending everything's fine when it's not, or acting like you don't care when you do), pause and ask yourself: "What would happen if I were honest about how I'm really feeling?" Take one small step toward vulnerability by sharing your true feelings with someone you trust.

Let Go of Control

A huge part of our armor is built around the need for control. We try to control our environment, our relationships, and even our own emotions in an attempt to avoid discomfort. But the truth is, life is unpredictable, and trying to control everything only leads to frustration and anxiety.

Letting go of control means accepting that you can't predict or manage everything that happens to you. It means trusting yourself and the process of life, even when things don't go according to plan.

Exercise: Pick one area of your life where you've been trying to maintain strict control (maybe it's your career, a relationship, or your future plans). Take a moment to reflect on how this need for control has been affecting you. How much stress and energy is it costing you? Now, practice letting go—just for today. Release the need to know the outcome, and trust that things will unfold as they're meant to.

▸ Immediate Action: Visualization for Letting Go

This exercise will help you let go of limiting beliefs, emotional burdens, and fears that have been weighing you down, using the power of visualization to facilitate emotional release.

Find a Quiet Space:

Start by finding a quiet, comfortable place where you won't be disturbed. Sit or lie down, close your eyes, and take a few deep breaths. Allow your body to relax fully, releasing any physical tension you may be holding onto.

Visualize Your Armor:

In your mind's eye, imagine yourself wearing a heavy suit of armor. This armor represents all the emotional burdens, fears, limiting beliefs, and past experiences that have been weighing you down. Notice the details of this armor—its weight, texture, and the way it restricts your movement. How does it feel to carry this armor with you every day?

Remove the Armor, Piece by Piece:

Now, begin to visualize yourself removing the armor, piece by piece. Start with the helmet—gently take it off and set it down. As you do, imagine releasing self-critical thoughts or beliefs about your self-worth that no longer serve you. Feel the lightness that comes with this first release.

Next, move to the chest plate, unfastening it and letting it fall away. This piece may represent fear or insecurity that's been guarding your heart. As you let go of this, breathe deeply and feel the openness in your chest.

Continue removing each part of the armor—the shoulder guards, arm plates, leg pieces—letting go of any old patterns, doubts, or fears attached to these pieces. As each piece falls away, feel your body becoming lighter, freer, and more open to possibility.

Feel the Freedom:

Once you've removed all the armor, take a moment to notice how your body feels. Imagine yourself standing tall, free from the weight of these old burdens. With every breath, feel the sense of freedom and peace that comes from releasing what no longer serves you.

Anchor This Feeling:

To solidify this experience, imagine wrapping yourself in a soft, light cloak of peace and self-compassion. This represents the new energy you want to carry forward—one of openness, trust, and self-acceptance.

Reflection and Integration:

After the visualization, take a few moments to reflect. What did each piece of armor represent for you? How does it feel to release these burdens?

As you move forward in your day, keep this feeling of lightness with you. Anytime you feel weighed down by fear, doubt, or stress, return to this exercise and visualize shedding the armor once more.

Questions for Reflection

- What are the pieces of "armor" you've been carrying? How do they protect you, and in what ways do they weigh you down?

- When was the last time you felt truly free and aligned with your authentic self? What circumstances allowed that to happen?

- How do your fears or limiting beliefs shape the choices you make in your daily life? Are they helping you, or keeping you stuck?

- What would your life look like if you started embracing vulnerability more often? How could this change your relationships or your self-view?

- In what areas of your life are you holding on too tightly to control? What might happen if you practiced letting go, even for a short time?

- How have external expectations—whether from family, society, or your own past experiences—shaped your self-identity? What parts of yourself might you need to reclaim or rediscover?

Conclusion: Embrace the Journey of Self-Exploration

Self-exploration isn't always easy—it requires courage, vulnerability, and a willingness to face the parts of ourselves we've been avoiding. But it's also one of the most rewarding journeys you'll ever take. As you peel back the layers and reconnect with your true self, you'll find a sense of freedom and peace that no external achievement can provide.

This journey is ongoing. There's no final destination where you'll suddenly know everything about yourself. But with each step you take, you'll become more aligned with your authentic self and less weighed down by the armor of fear, doubt, and societal expectations.

By embracing the process of self-exploration, you'll not only find personal liberation but also create a life that's more meaningful, joyful, and fulfilling. Your true self is waiting to be discovered—are you ready to meet them?

Final Reflection

True freedom is not found in perfection or control, but in the courage to strip away the armor, face your vulnerabilities, and accept yourself as you are.

The Beginning of Your Journey

As you reach this final chapter, it's important to recognize that this is not the end of the road—far from it. This is your beginning. Everything you've read, learned, and reflected on throughout these pages is merely the foundation of what's to come. You've unlocked new insights, discovered tools that can transform your life, and opened your mind to possibilities you might have never considered before. Now, it's time to take the next step: applying what you've learned and truly embracing the person you are destined to become.

It's easy to close a book and feel inspired for a moment. We've all been there. The real magic happens when you take that inspiration and use it to create lasting change. Imagine yourself not just reading about transformation but living it—feeling it in your daily actions, seeing it in the way you handle challenges, relationships, and opportunities. This is your moment to rise.

Why You Are Capable of Change

Right now, you might feel a surge of motivation, but perhaps there's also a hint of doubt creeping in. That little voice inside that whispers, "Can I really do this?" Let's silence that voice for a moment. You are capable of far more than you give yourself credit for. The potential for greatness isn't reserved for a select few; it's within every single one of us—including you.

Here's the truth: you don't need to be perfect to start making changes. You don't need to have all the answers or wait for the "right time." You simply need to begin. Every step, no matter how small, is progress. Every shift in mindset, no matter how subtle, is a win. The journey ahead may not always be easy, but it will be worth it. And the person you will become along the way? That's the true prize.

The Ripple Effect of Change

When you commit to becoming the best version of yourself, the impact extends far beyond you. Imagine the ripple effect. The changes you make in your own life—whether it's improving your mindset, pursuing your dreams, or deepening your relationships—will inspire and uplift others.

You will be a light for those around you, showing them what's possible when someone takes control of their life and chooses growth over fear. This doesn't mean you need to be perfect. As we talked, vulnerability, mistakes, and imperfections are all part of the journey. But when you step forward with courage, others will see that they, too, can do the same.

Think about the people in your life—your friends, your family, your community. What kind of example do you want to set for them? By stepping into your greatness, you give others permission to do the same. Your courage will become contagious.

Embrace the Process

If there's one thing to remember as you close this book, it's this: fall in love with the process. Don't get so focused on the destination that you forget to enjoy the journey. There will be highs and lows, victories and setbacks, but through it all, you'll grow stronger, wiser, and more resilient.

Celebrate the small wins. Take time to reflect on how far you've come, even if the progress seems slow. Every step forward is still a step forward. Be kind to yourself along the way. Personal growth isn't a straight line, and you don't need to have everything figured out right away. Give yourself permission to be a work in progress.

Success isn't about achieving a specific goal—it's about who you become in the pursuit of that goal. It's about the lessons you learn, the courage you build, and the resilience you develop. Every challenge you face is an opportunity to grow stronger, and every obstacle is a chance to prove to yourself that you are capable of more than you ever imagined.

You Already Have Everything You Need

One of the most empowering realizations is this: you already have everything you need to succeed within you. The knowledge, the strength, the creativity—it's all there. The journey you've been on, and the tools you've learned, have simply helped you uncover it.

There's no need to wait for external validation or for someone to give you permission to pursue your dreams. You are the author of your own story, and the pen is firmly in your hand. From this moment forward, you get to decide how your story unfolds.

When doubt creeps in, remind yourself that you are enough as you are right now. There's no need to chase perfection or wait until you feel completely ready. Take imperfect action, embrace the learning curve, and trust that every step forward is moving you closer to your dreams.

Your Next Steps

As you set out on this new chapter of your life, here are a few final thoughts to keep in mind:

Start Small: You don't need to overhaul your entire life overnight. Focus on one or two areas where you can begin to implement what you've learned. Over time, small, consistent actions will lead to big results.

Be Patient: Change takes time, and personal growth is a lifelong journey. Be patient with yourself, and don't be discouraged by setbacks. Remember, every step forward is progress.

Trust the Process: The journey won't always be easy, but it will always be worth it. Trust that the challenges you face are shaping you into the person you're meant to be.

Celebrate Your Wins: Don't forget to acknowledge your progress along the way. Celebrate the small victories, and use them as motivation to keep going.

A Final Thought: The Power is in Your Hands

As you close this book, you're standing on the edge of something extraordinary. The power to transform your life is in your hands, and it has been all along. You've learned the tools, gained the insights, and now it's time to apply them.

The best part? You're ready. You may not feel like it at every moment, but you have everything you need to begin. Trust yourself, believe in your potential, and take that first step.

Here's to your next chapter—the one where you step into your greatness, live authentically, and create a life that lights you up from the inside out.

Now go out there and write your awesome story!

A Personalized Action Plan

Now that you've explored the key principles for success and personal growth, it's time to take action. Below is a simple outline to help you create a personalized action plan. Use it as a guide to turn your dreams into reality, one step at a time.

1. Define Your Most Important Goals

Take a moment to reflect on the areas of your life where you want to see change or growth. Write down your top three goals. These could be personal, professional, financial, or related to your health and well-being.

Goal 1: _____

Goal 2: _____

Goal 3: _____

2. Break Them Down into Achievable Actions

Once you've defined your goals, break each one into smaller, actionable steps. Think of these as daily or weekly tasks that move you closer to your bigger goal.

Goal 1:

Action 1: _____

Action 2: _____

Action 3: _____

Goal 2:

Action 1: _____

Action 2: _____

Action 3: _____

Goal 3:

Action 1: _____

Action 2: _____

Action 3: _____

3. Set Follow-Up Dates and Evaluate Your Progress

Commit to reviewing your progress regularly. Choose dates to check in on how you're doing, assess what's working, and make adjustments where needed. Write down your follow-up dates.

Progress Check for Goal 1: _____

Progress Check for Goal 2: _____

Progress Check for Goal 3: _____

The key is to stay flexible. Your goals might evolve over time, and that's perfectly fine. The important thing is to keep moving forward and to celebrate every small victory along the way.

Your personalized action plan is your map—use it to guide you on your journey towards achieving your dreams!

www.ingramcontent.com/pod-product-compliance
Lightning Source LLC
LaVergne TN
LVHW041907070526
838199LV00051BA/2531